OVERCOMING

SCHOOL REFUSAL

A practical guide
for teachers, counsellors,
caseworkers and parents

JOANNE GARFI

AUSTRALIANACADEMICPRESS

First published 2018 by:
Australian Academic Press Group Pty. Ltd.
18 Victor Russell Drive
Samford Valley QLD 4520, Australia
www.australianacademicpress.com.au

Overcoming School Refusal: A practical guide for teachers, counsellors,
caseworkers and parents

ISBN   9781925644043 (paperback)
ISBN   9781925644050 (ebook)

Publisher: Stephen May
Copy editing: Rhonda McPherson
Cover design: Luke Harris, Working Type Studio
Typesetting: Australian Academic Press
Printing: Lightning Source

Contents

Acknowledgements

The idea for this book came as something of an epiphany during a road trip with a friend in 2017 and has only become a reality with the help and support of some very special people. Firstly, I would like to thank my daughters and husband who never once doubted I could do this even though I had many, many doubts and fears. Special thanks also go to my publisher and co-conspirator Stephen May who could see the potential in this book and said so from day one. Stephen, you will never know how much that first conversation we had meant to me. Thank you for believing in me and guiding me through to this point. You have been amazing. I'd also like to thank my dear friend and mentor Dr Angela Ramagnano who offered support and encouragement when I felt like I was fraying at the edges. You have been an earth angel since the day I met you. Finally, but certainly not least, I would like to thank the families and students who have enriched my knowledge by allowing me to work with them. All the theories, differential diagnoses and treatment modalities mean nothing if you do not have the right people to work with and learn from. This book is for you and all the 'you' that I will meet in the future. Together we can do this!

Joanne Garfi is a psychologist with over 30 years of experience and expertise in child and adolescent issues. She has 9 years' experience as a school psychologist, working in both primary and secondary schools providing specialised training to teachers. She has a special interest in the treatment of anxiety and panic disorder and is well known for her work with childhood anxiety, behavioural disorders and developmental issues. She currently conducts workshops on school refusal around Australia. Joanne uses a variety of treatment modalities and prefers to take a whole person approach to treatment. Her emphasis when working with children is to have families and schools working together to bring about change.

Chapter 1

What is school refusal?

School refusal is a complex issue that is stressful for the child, their family and the school. The more time a child is away from school, the more difficult it is for the child to resume normal school life. If school refusal becomes an ongoing issue it can negatively impact the child's social and educational development.

Children who develop school refusal display severe emotional and cognitive stress in the face of attending school. While it is a well established behavioural condition, it is not recognised as a disorder in its own right within the main diagnostic tool used by psychologists and psychiatrists to reliably diagnose disorders — the *Diagnostic and Statistical Manual of Mental Disorders*, 5th edition (DSM-5).[1] There is, however, a consensus in the literature that school refusal is characterised by absences from school that can be over extended periods of time, periodic, general tardiness or repeated missed classes. It is driven by intense feelings of anxiety that can arise from a variety of causes, which we will discuss further in future chapters.

In contrast to the issue of truancy, an anxious child who refuses to attend school does so because they are genuinely distressed. A school refuser will often attempt to get up in the morning, put on their uniform, have breakfast and may even make it to the car or the school drop-off zone but when the time comes to take those fateful last steps they either become angry and defiant or tearful and distressed. The school refuser makes no secret of their inability to attend school. They will often say that they want to go to school but can't.

This is in marked contrast to the truant whose absences are not anxiety-based and who hides the fact that they are not attending school. Unlike the school refuser the truant will engage in alternate behaviours when not at school, such as spending the day with friends, shopping or walking the streets of the city.

Parents of school refusers often report overt anxiety symptoms shortly after the child gets home from school. Parents report a variety of symptoms including moodiness, aggressive outbursts, unwillingness to complete homework, reduced appetite, excessive worry, changes in sleep patterns and reluctance to engage in bedtime routines as it signals the end of the day and the imminent start of another school day. These symptoms are often worse on Sunday nights and a day or two before the beginning of a new school term as the child has had several days away from school and has had time to distance themselves from the anxiety associated with going to school. Many parents dread the beginning of a new term for this very reason.

Anxiety and school refusal

In order to best understand school refusal we must have a solid understanding of child anxiety. Up to 80% of school refusers meet criteria for some form of anxiety disorder whether it be separation anxiety, generalised anxiety or social anxiety.[2]

According to the DSM-5, anxiety is the anticipation of future threat, while fear is the emotional response to a real or perceived imminent threat. Although these two states overlap they also differ in that fear is more often associated with surges of autonomic arousal necessary for the fight or flight response, while anxiety is more often associated with muscle tension and vigilance in preparation for a future danger. While anxiety disorders (separation anxiety disorder, generalised anxiety disorder and social anxiety disorder) have a high rate of comorbidity, they can be differentiated by examination of the types of situations that are feared or avoided. Separation anxiety is at its core a fear of being separated from a significant person who is believed to offer comfort, safety and support. Social anxiety is characterised by marked fear or anxiety about one or more social situations in which the individual is exposed to possible scrutiny by others. Generalised anxiety disorder, on the other hand, is characterised by excessive worrying about a number of events or activities. For the purposes of simplicity I will use the umbrella term 'anxiety disorder' throughout this book and where necessary will venture into specific anxiety disorders as the need arises.

Anxiety disorder is a commonly occurring mental health disorder that affects approximately 14% of the population[3] or one in seven people, which means that we all know at least one or two people who suffer with this disorder. Its severity can range from mild (where the person can still attend school/work), right through to severe (where the person is challenged to leave their home). It is characterised by persistent, excessive worry that hinders logical thinking and action. Individuals with anxiety disorder typically overestimate the perceived danger in situations and become either overly cautious or avoidant. In the case of school refusal, the child has often experienced a negative situation at school (i.e., bullying, failed assessment task) and avoids a reoccurrence of the incident by avoiding school. The longer the child is away the greater the perceived danger becomes causing symptoms to become ever more severe. Symptoms as listed in the DSM-5 are typically characterised by restlessness, being easily fatigued, difficulty concentrating, irritability, muscle tension, and sleep disturbance.

This does not mean that the remaining 86% of the population are anxiety-free as anxiety is part of everyday life. Think, for example, of the last time you attended the dentist or entered a meeting with your employer, which you suspected, would not end well. That dread, that hollow sick feeling in your stomach, the clammy hands, the racing thoughts, the tightness in your throat and chest, is your body telling you that your anxiety is on the rise and that you are not coping. Anxiety can also be triggered by everyday occurrences like the traffic on the way to work, arguments with our loved ones, and children who will not get ready for school. For most people (86%) these feelings of distress/anxiety/stress will subside once the situation is resolved but for some (14%) this return to equilibrium is not easily achieved. For these people everything that goes wrong in their day (no matter how small) adds to the existing high levels of anxiety until eventually the body can take no more and a panic attack ensues. Yep that's right: a panic attack doesn't just come out of nowhere, it is a result of persistent anxiety that builds and results in an abrupt surge of intense fear or discomfort that leads to panic symptoms. So, your child's frenzied tantrum at 8 am has been building for hours and sometimes even days. A panic attack is the body's way of saying 'too much stress, can't manage it any more, let's get rid of it'. That is why, after a panic attack, the sufferer often reports feeling tired, sleepy and worn out. A panic attack is the emotional equivalent of a pressure cooker with a blocked outlet valve.

Now imagine these intense feelings in a child who has been worried about going to school since the day before (obvious signs of not coping often begin around dinner time) and suddenly it's not surprising that they lash out at the well-meaning parent or carer who is trying to get them to school.

Fear (which is what the child feels when they're told they're going to school) provokes a fight, flight, or freeze response. The child will either argue back, lash out and flee to their room or the playground area, (if at school), or say nothing and have rivers of tears flowing down their cheeks. This is normally where parents become frustrated, angry or completely disheartened and eventually give into the child's pleas resulting in another day off school and more feelings of failure for everyone involved. Every day that a parent or caregiver gives into the child's pleas and reasons for not attending school, we reinforce their fear and teach the child that the louder they scream, the harder they plead and the more plausible their reasons, the more likely we are to give in. This does not mean that the child is innately devious or manipulative, they are simply using whatever is at their disposal to achieve their desired goal: not going to school and hence reducing their level of distress. Rather than allowing this self-destructive behaviour to continue we, as service providers and parents, need to provide the child with the knowledge and skills to recognise their symptoms of anxiety and manage them in a way that empowers and rebuilds self-esteem.

A good analogy of this would be teaching a child to swim. Initially the child is afraid of the water, especially if they have had a bad experience, and may cry and cling to the parent as they enter the water. Their instincts are to hold on to their carer for dear life. If the carer does not encourage the child to begin to let go, it is highly likely that the child will never learn to swim and may in fact develop a real fear of water. However, if the carer reassures the child and tolerates their cries and praises even the slightest of achievements the child begins to **believe** that they are capable. Progress will, of course, be very slow but if every time the carer gets into the pool there is an **expectation** that the child will pick up where they left off the last lesson progress **will** begin to occur.

Just as the swimmer is slowly **encouraged** and **expected** to master their water skills so must we **expect** the school refuser to return to school. It is important that we all understand that the school refuser will not miraculously get up one day having mastered their anxiety and gladly go to school. Learning to master their anxiety symptoms comes from learning what anxiety is, how it presents, what can be done to control it and real-life exposure that is done at a pace the child can handle. Just like the swimmer, we must always expect that the following day will be a slight improvement on the day before. This is how empowerment and self-esteem is built no matter what the challenge may be.

Returning a child to school can be a monumental task taking enormous time and energy on the part of parents, teachers, psychologists and of course the child (who may initially not like any of these people very much). The early stages of returning a child to school can be a thankless and heart wrenching ordeal but an integrated team approach can produce positive, long-term outcomes as I have evidenced in my 30 years as a psychologist.

What does school refusal look like?

Let's look at an example of school refusal compiled from multiple case studies:

> Jacqui is an 11-year-old girl who has attended the same primary school for 6 years. She has a good group of friends, gets on well with teachers and is doing well academically. Six months prior to referral Jacqui injures her foot resulting in surgery and approximately three months off school.
>
> During her recuperation, Jacqui is forced to stop her beloved dancing and limit outings with friends as walking becomes a challenge. In an effort to support Jacqui, her mother (Bianca) takes time off work. For the first time since beginning school Jacqui spends most days with Bianca while her siblings are at school. Bianca reports that Jacqui remained in touch with friends via social media and telephone calls but had very little face-to-face contact during her time away from school.

As Jacqui's injury improved Bianca began leaving Jacqui with family and friends so she could return to work. This coincided with Jacqui reporting tummy upsets, headaches and nausea immediately after dinner on days when her mother was due to go to work the following morning. Jacqui would beg her mother not to go to work. To her mother's credit she never gave in to Jacqui's pleas but did admit to feeling very guilty and sad at having to leave her.

Just as Jacqui began to settle into staying with grandparents or family friends, her physiotherapist announced that a return to school would be achievable within a week or two. Almost immediately Jacqui's symptoms worsened ten-fold. Her parents reported uncontrolled bouts of anger, tears, tummy upsets, headaches, broken sleep and variable appetite.

The night before her scheduled return to school Jacqui complains of aches and pains, sore tummy, difficulty breathing and sleeping. By the time Jacqui is woken the following morning she is red-eyed and crying uncontrollably, begging and pleading with her parents to give her ONE more day at home. She assures them that the following day will be different and that she just needs the day to adjust. But guess what? The next day was no better, nor the day after that, nor the week after that. When I met Jacqui she had been absent from school for a total of two school terms.

The three major factors of school refusal — FEAR + ANXIETY + AVOIDANCE — are well illustrated in this case example. Jacqui develops a **fear** of returning to school following an injury. But why did the fear develop? Let's think carefully about what happened when Jacqui injured herself: she lost face-to-face contact with friends, stopped dancing, missed school work, developed bad habits (i.e., not needing to follow a morning routine), and got loads of attention from mum while she was recovering. Returning to school became a challenge because Jacqui had lost self-confidence and experienced lots of secondary gains that made being at home comfortable and nonchallenging. She did not believe she could return to school because she had missed so much schoolwork, lost contact with her peers and was afraid she could not fit in as she had before her accident.

Once fear sets in **anxiety** quickly follows and grows exponentially as anxiety is fed by fear. In fact, anxiety is, at its very root, a fear of fear (in other words, Jacqui became afraid of being afraid). Once fear and anxiety are present, **avoidance** is highly likely to develop, as no-one (irrespective of age or gender) will willingly place themselves in a situation that provokes fear and anxiety.

Once in place, school refusal is driven by one or more of the following reasons:

- **Avoiding situations that evoke negative emotions.** 'If I don't go to school I don't need to explain my absence or feel stupid because I've missed so much work'.
- **Escape from negative social and/or evaluative situations.** For example, bullying or receiving exam results.
- **Attention seeking.** 'When I don't go to school mum stays home with me or I go to grandma's house and everyone wants to know what's wrong with me'.
- **Rewards.** 'Once I'm home I don't have to do schoolwork, I can watch TV, eat whatever I like and keep in touch with friends using social media'.

Determining what 'drives' school refusal is an integral part of beginning to understand the child, and developing a program that is specifically geared to their particular situation. The child who refuses to go to school because they love being at home with mum needs a very different return to school program than the child who refuses to go to school because they are mercilessly bullied.

How common is school refusal?

Although research has struggled to provide a consistent school refusal figure, due to differing opinions on what constitutes school refusal behaviours and when school absences cross the line from acceptable to unacceptable, there seems to be a consensus that school refusal occurs in 1% to 5 % of all children.[4]

It peaks from the ages of 5 to 7 and then again from the ages of 11 to 14. These ages correspond directly to transition periods. That is, the years when children go from kinder (where they only spend a few hours per week) to primary school (where they are present for full days, 5 days per week) and then again when the child goes from primary school to secondary school where academic demands become greater and social relationships become more complex. Transition periods occur throughout our lives and have varying degrees of impact on our emotional well being.

Our first transition period is often moving from mother's care to kinder or day care. For the sensitive anxious child this transition can trigger lots of anxiety and manifest as clinginess, poor sleep (often resulting in co sleeping), altered eating patterns, tantrums and refusing activities that require separation from mother. This anxiety is referred to as separation anxiety and is a normal part of development.

Separation anxiety is first noted in infancy when the child reacts negatively to the mother leaving the room or the child being handed to someone else to hold. This need to be with the mother is a normal part of our survival instinct as the baby fears abandonment. Crying and screaming is their attempt, at an instinctual level, to ensure connection with the person who feeds and nurtures them. We see this in the animal kingdom, as well, when offspring cry out for their mother to make her aware that they have been left unattended.

In the nonanxious child this fear of being separated from the mother declines as they become familiar with their environment and begin to trust their new caregivers. Most of us know at least one child who has called their kinder teacher or child carer 'mum'. A sure sign that the child trusts that person to care for them. The anxious child, however, tends to take longer to settle into their new environment and remains untrusting of their carers. It is not unusual for parents of school refusers to report problems with their child settling into kinder or day care. The re-emergence of their anxiety at the start of school coincides with a new environment, new carers, longer hours, more academic and social demands and, most importantly, longer periods of separation from mother. As a rule we would expect the anxiety to settle within a week or two as the environment becomes familiar and would expect that, by age 7, this fear of being separated from their primary care giver would have ended. Separation anxiety beyond the age of 7 is not considered a normal part of development and is viewed as the beginning of a diagnosable anxiety disorder.

Other transition periods in our lives include moving from primary school to secondary school, secondary school to university or work, leaving the family home to live alone or with a partner, and retirement to name a few. For the clinically anxious person, each of these transition periods equates to a period of instability and stress that extends beyond what would normally be accepted as a 'settling-in period'.

School refusal occurs across all socioeconomic groups. This means that whether the child is from an affluent family in a private school or a less privileged family in a public school, school refusal can and does develop. It is also equally prevalent amongst boys and girls.

In summary then:

- School refusal can occur in any family and any school. In a medium-sized school of 500 students you would expect between 5 and 25 students to experience some level of school refusal.
- School refusers have often had difficulties settling into kinder and/or day care.

- School refusal does not end when school ends as clinical levels of anxiety will resurface whenever transition periods occur.

- School refusal is just as common in girls as it is in boys.

Given the frequency of school refusal and the far reaching implications that it holds for the individual, family and school community, it is essential that time and funds are made available for training and treatment of this difficult and complex issue which we are often ill equipped to manage.

Types of school refusers

School refusers can be grouped into three types: anxious/separation anxiety; anxious/depressed, and phobic school refusers.

Anxious/separation anxiety

This group is mainly characterised by younger children transitioning from kinder to school. We would expect anxiety to diminish as the child becomes accustomed to their environment and should be absent by age 7 when developmental separation anxiety will have been outgrown.

Case example

Sienna is a 5½-year-old prep student who is referred by the family general practitioner (GP) for treatment of separation anxiety that has been present since beginning kindergarten but has become significantly worse since beginning school. Sienna's mother (Annette) explains that she is a stay-at-home mum with a 2-year-old child, who has only worked intermittently since Sienna's birth. When not in her mother's care Sienna has been in her maternal grandmother's care whom she loves very much. Sienna is reported as having had separation anxiety when she first started kinder but this subsided within the first term. Since beginning primary school, Sienna is reported as having difficulty falling asleep and staying asleep, changes in eating patterns, highly anxious, prone to aggressive outbursts and intolerant of her younger sibling. Annette reports tears and tantrums from the minute she is dropped off at her classroom. Annette admits that there have been several mornings where Sienna has become so distressed that she has allowed her to remain at home. Sienna is typical of many first-year students who struggle with the individuation required to successfully commence school. She has managed kinder but only after repeated exposures and is now struggling with full days at school where she cannot be with her mother, grandmother or sibling. A program tailored to her specific needs with emphasis on developing independence and understanding, rewarding progress and encouraging exposure should produce quick and long lasting changes. We would expect that by the end of the second term, Sienna will have adjusted to her environment and developed enough independence to accept her mother's absence. If, however, Sienna was still exhibiting extreme levels of anxiety by the end of her first year and into her second year of school we would begin to question the reason for this and perhaps refer her to a paediatrician for a second opinion.

Anxious/depressed group

This group is mainly characterised by older students who may have had a history of separation anxiety in early childhood and experienced varying degrees of success in attending school.

Where a previous history has not been present the school refusal may have been triggered by a life event (for example, bullying, school change, parental split). Unlike the anxious school refuser this group (in addition to anxiety symptoms) exhibit depressive symptoms that could include:

- lethargy (lack of energy, motivation and overpowering drowsiness or sleep)
- anhedonia (an inability to experience pleasure from things that had previously been joyful; e.g., playing football)
- diminished ability to think clearly or concentrate,
- depressed mood or irritability often described as a feeling of sadness or emptiness
- suicidal ideation or plan
- significant weight loss or weight gain

- feelings of worthlessness

- excessive, unwarranted guilt.

This group will often cause parents and teachers enormous concern as their demeanour is flat and negative leading to fears for their well being. It can be very difficult to engage parents to re-motivate this group as they fear that even the slightest push to get their child back to school could lead to self-harm.

Case example

> Riley is a 13-year-old boy who attends a local secondary school and is referred for school refusal by his GP. Riley is the eldest of two children and the son of a nurse and mechanic, who both work long hours. Family dynamics are assessed as loving and supportive. Riley informs me at our first session that he was bullied in primary school intermittently for his weight but also for his bowel condition which meant that he could occasionally smell. Although his condition is significantly better and smell is no longer an issue he is still very sensitive to body odour and showers a minimum of two times per day. He admits to exaggerating symptoms when he was younger to get out of school but denies that he is doing so now. His mother reports that Riley has not attended school for six weeks and has stopped attending cricket training, withdrawn from friends and spends most of his time in his room playing computer games. When encouraged to participate in family celebrations Riley becomes aggressive and rude until he is given permission to not be involved. Riley's parents report that Riley occasionally expresses a desire to be dead, which frightens them and dissuades them from pushing the school attendance issue. Riley claims that his refusal to attend school comes from his immense lethargy and fear that he'll fall asleep in class and be bullied by other students. Secretly I am informed by Riley's year level coordinator that Riley was rejected by a girl in his year level, which may have been the catalyst for the school refusal.

As we can see, Riley's case study is significantly more complex than Sienna's, and includes symptoms that clearly suggest the presence of depression. Re-establishing healthy daily routines, encouraging reconnection with friends and assessing the need for medication would be among our first priorities. It would be fair to assume that Riley will take longer to be re-integrated but this is still completely achievable.

There is often an overrepresentation of students diagnosed with autism spectrum disorder (ASD) in this group, as is also the case for high achieving/perfectionistic students. Both groups will be discussed in detail in Chapters 7 and 8.

Phobic school refusers

As the name suggests, this group has often had a long history of school refusal with varying degrees of success in re-engagement, and is characterised by older students. This group rarely makes an attempt to get to school and parents rarely try to motivate them on a consistent basis. Parents will often report bouts of yelling and screaming but rarely is there a systematic and consistent approach. This group can be quite complacent knowing that the family has been worn down and will only lash out when forced to make change.

Families of this group are often burnt out and can present as unmotivated, sceptical or resistant. These families require as much (if not more) support than their child as they too need to learn to overcome their anxiety and remain strong in the face of adversity.

Case example

Some years ago I met the parents of a 14-year-old boy (Charles), who had been referred to me by child protection services, for assistance in getting their son back to school. The parents informed me that they worked long hours and had three sons all of whom had, at some point in their education, refused to attend school. They described their many attempts to get their eldest son back to school and spoke of the frustration, anger and heartache they felt when, after much intervention by professionals, school and parents, they were only able to get him back to school for the fourth term of Year 10. At the time of referral they informed me that their eldest son was in his early twenties and unemployed. He had lost contact with most of his friends and tended to stay in his room playing computer games and watching TV. Not surprisingly there was some question of whether this son suffered with depression.

To add to their despair, their middle son also disengaged from school. The parents admitted to making only a half-hearted attempt at getting him back to school given the turmoil the family had experienced with their eldest son. As with his older brother, this son was also unemployed and very much confined to the family home. Their middle son was in his late teens at the time of referral.

It was of no surprise to me that their youngest son, Charles, had followed his elder brothers' footsteps given that he had watched his parents take the path of least resistance particularly with his middle brother. When I met with Charles, he presented as a respectful and quiet young man who was genuinely distressed when we discussed a possible return to school. Charles admitted to disliking school and feeling out of place when he attended. He understandably preferred to be at home with his two older brothers, who would occasionally include him in one of their computer games.

Charles had scarcely attended school since the start of secondary school with periods of nonattendance reported in primary school. His parents admitted to leaving for work without even attempting to get him out of bed as they were fed up with the arguments, which were ultimately fruitless.

There is no doubt that Charles's anxiety about going to school was very real but we must remember that Charles had not really been **expected** to attend school for some time. By the time I met Charles and his parents, the fear of going to school had become so great that avoidance was the only solution. Or to use an old adage: 'Charles had come off the horse and had never really been expected to get back on'. Hence he had forgotten how to 'ride'.

It was only with the involvement of his school, extensive education of his parents about anxiety/fear/ avoidance and clear expectations of Charles that we were able to slowly get him back to limited school hours.

Sadly, Charles and his family moved away before we were able to complete his return to school. I often wonder what happened to Charles and his brothers and use their story in presentations as an example of what happens when issues are not addressed in their infancy and parents become despondent. In this case, what started as a problem with one child became a scourge for an entire family. As with all phobias, the longer we take to begin the exposure process the more difficult it becomes to challenge and successfully eradicate the phobia.

Chapter 2

Why do children refuse to go to school?

Children refuse to go to school for many reasons. It is important, where possible, that we try to identify the factors that lead to the disengagement. The factors discussed in this chapter are in no way exhaustive, but may help narrow down the possible causes.

Fearing the loss of a parent

We often see this fear occur when a child has been separated from a parent (or parents) due to hospitalisation or when one parent has left the family home for an extended period of time and then returns (i.e., to serve in the military). As our natural instincts are to remain close to our parents, as they are directly responsible for our survival, we cling to that parent once they return for fear that they will leave again. In the nonclinically anxious child, this fear of loss passes as the child slowly comes to realise that the parent is no longer at risk of leaving. However, for the clinically anxious child this fear remains and affects their ability to engage in normal daily activities that require separation from that parent. Family breakdown can also create this fear of loss as the child fears that their remaining parent will also leave.

Needing to protect a parent

Children also need to know that their parents are safe. If a child has witnessed or heard family violence, their fear for the abused parent will escalate. Remaining at home, especially if the abuser is at home during school hours (due to unemployment or shift work), is one way to minimise the threat. The child, in effect, takes on the role of protector. Alternatively, the child may stay at home in the belief that they can help a sick or grieving parent; therefore, becoming the parent's nurse or counsellor. For example, a child may stay at home to keep mum company after parents have separated because they have seen mum cry when she is alone but perk up when she sees the child.

Jealousy

School refusal can be brought on by jealousy. This is especially true if another sibling is at home for health reasons and is seen to be having fun while they recuperate. A good example of this might be: a sibling being at home with chickenpox and mum taking time off work to care for the sick child. The child attending school then discovers that mum has been baking goodies and playing with the sick child while the well child is expected to go to school. Becoming 'sick and anxious' is a nice way of joining in on the fun. Similarly visitors from interstate or overseas can trigger the desire to spend more time at home with them, especially if parents or older siblings have taken time off work.

Family dysfunction

Dysfunction within the family could include parents arguing, older siblings or parents with mental health or physical ailments, an unemployed parent who is lonely, or a pet that is sick. Whether real or perceived the child believes that remaining at home will help alleviate these issues; therefore, the child will create symptoms that facilitate their carer role.

Transition

Any change from old and comfortable to new and challenging can produce very high levels of anxiety particularly for the clinically anxious child. For example, moving to a new school and leaving behind well-known teachers, friends and surroundings can produce such turmoil and distress that the child cannot bring themselves to start anew. This is why appropriate care must be taken when children are involved in a major life transition. Where possible, the child should be encouraged to visit their new school several times and be provided with buddies who will communicate on a regular basis to help the child integrate more easily once they move to their new school. Letters of welcome, video calls from students and teachers can make this transition significantly less stressful and even enjoyable. If the transition is to a new home then the child should be involved and included in moving and setting up their room. This process eases the child into their new surroundings and produces less stress.

Recent illness

The illness could be short or long term. Sometimes a week off school with a cold can be enough to trigger an unwillingness to return to school, especially if predisposing issues were already present before the illness. For example, poor grades, bullying, or fights with a best friend. Get well cards from classmates, phone calls from the class teacher, visits from school friends, can all go a long way towards making the return to school more pleasurable. Where complex issues exist, every effort should be made to rectify these before the child returns to school. Extra help for poor grades must be provided, bullying issues must be addressed, and friendship issues resolved. A return to school may still be stressful but if all known issues have been addressed this stress should be short lived.

Being bullied

Bullying is an important school refusal factor to investigate carefully as children will often not tell teachers or parents that they are being bullied for fear of retribution when the bully is confronted. It is our role as parents and carers to be aware of subtle changes in the child that could suggest bullying. For example, is the child exhibiting:

- suddenly walking around the school alone at recess and lunch or seen hiding away in toilets or the library
- soiling or wetting pants, especially in younger children
- onset of sleep disturbance
- weight loss or weight gain
- unexplained bouts of crying or aggressive outbursts
- difficulty concentrating in class
- showing overt fear/anxiety when the bell for recess and lunchtime sounds.

We need to remember that staying home and facing a parent's wrath is easier than having to face more bullying. Bully busting strategies as suggested by Evelyn Field in her book *Bully Busting*[1] might be a good place to start if bullying is suspected as the underlying cause for school refusal.

Not having friends

Children may tell parents they have many friends but in reality will walk around the schoolyard alone because they have fought with friends or struggle to make friends. This is especially true of children diagnosed with ASD as they often have difficulty reading social situations and are unsure of how one goes about making and keeping a friend. The introduction of friendship groups at recess and lunch breaks can help all these children and can reflect popular activities at the time (e.g., a fidget spinner championship, an Australian Ninja obstacle course, a chess club, a gardening group), anything that encourages children to congregate together and discuss a common activity. Social Skills groups are also helpful and although we often believe that Social Skills groups are reserved for children with ASD they can be just as effective with shy, anxious children who lack the confidence and skills to make friends. While it is important for parents to ask about their child's playmates and daily interactive activities, it is equally important that teachers on lunch and recess duty be mindful not only of the loud and disruptive child in the playground but also of the child who is timid and withdrawn and causes no disruption but is at risk of disengagement.

Not getting on with a teacher

Although teachers do their utmost to get along with all students, clashes of personality do occur. It may be possible that a particular teaching style does not work well with the school refuser's personality or there is a history of conflict between teacher and student. As one would expect, this is more common in older students and is often evidenced by the student attending class on the days they DO NOT have their disliked teacher. If this is the likely cause, it may be wise to consider a class change or encourage open discussion between the teacher and student with support people present for both the student and teacher.

Learning deficits

School is supposed to be challenging and engaging but for the child with learning deficits, school can become a nightmare. Struggling to understand concepts and keep up with class demands is a common reason for children to disengage from school. Parents and teachers will often overlook the possibility of learning deficits if the child has previously been on par with peers, but we must keep in mind that deficits can sometimes be hidden until the child's ability is exceeded by demand. In these cases a comprehensive educational assessment before re-engagement in school could aid to identify deficit areas and make a return to school more rewarding.

Fitting in

An extended holiday with family or period of illness may invite feelings of fear in the child when they are expected to seamlessly reintegrate into their class and school. Imagine, as an adult, returning to your workplace after a month or two off work and finding that systems have changed and work colleagues have regrouped. Now imagine that sick, hollow feeling in a child. It is suddenly not so surprising that they struggle to return to school. Staying in touch with teachers and students with letters, postcards, phone calls, video chat, warm fuzzies (short notes from each class member saying something nice about the child and why they want them back) are all part of easing the child's re-integration into their class.

Chapter 3

The impacts of school refusal

Physical, social and emotional

Physical symptoms

The physical symptoms expressed by a child who is refusing to attend school can be overwhelming for everyone involved. Parents will often report that the severity of symptoms is what ultimately convinces them to acquiesce. If, however, we understand that these physical symptoms are a normal part of panic and not life threatening, it becomes easier to assist the child work through the symptoms rather than giving in and allowing him/her to stay home. The physical symptoms typically witnessed include:

- headache
- emotional lability
- abdominal pain
- nausea
- shakiness
- dizziness
- hot/cold flushes
- racing heart
- difficulty breathing
- sore throat

- increased urination
- diarrhoea
- disturbed sleep patterns
- eye strain/eye ache.

These symptoms will normally subside once the child is confident that they will not be forced to attend school. Many parents will know the frustration of racing their child to the doctor with what appears to be a serious health issue only to be told that there is no organic basis for the symptoms and that the child has had a panic attack.

As important as it is for parents to learn to recognise panic symptoms, it is equally important for schools to be able to identify them as well. All too often parents will diligently work with their child in the morning to facilitate a timely arrival to school only to be called an hour or two later by the school and instructed to come pick the child up and take them home. While I am aware that schools are busy places with little time to spare, it is important that they too learn to recognise the child's panic symptoms and assist them without necessitating a call to parents.

In calling parents we, as service providers, are reinforcing the child's failure and ensuring that the following morning will be even harder for both the parent and child. We will discuss what professionals can do in Chapter 4.

Social consequences

It is perhaps not surprising that the consequences of school refusal are far-reaching and not limited to the physical symptoms experienced the night before or the morning of a school day. The reality is that the longer the school refuser is absent from school the more socially isolated they become. We all know that our social connectedness comes from our regular contact with those people we deem as friends. While social media may help facilitate some social contact, it cannot and should not replace face-to-face contact. It has been my experience that the school refuser may initially continue contact using social media or phone calls but as friends begin to question their protracted absence, the school refuser begins to distance themselves in order to avoid answering questions. As time passes these friends begin to regroup and begin engaging in activities that do not include the school refuser, as they are not present to be involved in the planning. As news filters down to the school refuser that their best friend(s) is engaging in activities that exclude them, the sadness and isolation begins and their feelings of being on the periphery become stronger. From here we begin to see the slow and gradual decline of the child's emotional well being until, like the case of Charles and his brothers from Chapter 1, the child (younger or older) retracts into themselves and finds solace in computer games and their online 'friends' who also play the game and ask no questions.

Emotional impact

As the time away from school increases we often begin to see an increase in emotional lability. Parents will often report that their child becomes overly concerned with what peers are thinking and saying about them and that they alternate between being tearful and angry. We also begin to see the emergence of self-doubt and a decline in self-esteem as they begin to feel more and more on the periphery with school friends and schoolwork. Generalised worry can also begin to rise as the child has lots of time on their hands to worry about the 'what ifs' in life; for example, fears for family members and overthinking world events. As the generalised worry escalates so too does the child's need to control their environment resulting in behaviour that can appear quite obsessive, such as demanding to know where family members are, what they are doing, and what the day ahead holds for every member of the family.

As we can see the consequences of not intervening in the early stages of school refusal have a profound impact on every aspect of the child's life.

As parents, teachers and service providers it is our role to ensure that this debilitating issue does not overtake the child's normal growth and development.

Short-term and long-term consequences

The consequences of protracted absences from school are far reaching and life changing. They not only impact the child's life but that of their family and are not limited to the child's education. If a child cannot get themselves to school how do they learn to manage work situations or adult relationships? So many of the skills we learn in childhood form the basis for adult behaviour. School attendance is one such skill that cannot be replaced. Whether we love our jobs or hate them we, as adults, must have the resilience and stamina to get up every morning and face another day as a worker. If we learnt in childhood that we could circumvent our responsibilities as a student we then expect the same will be the case in the workplace and, as we all know, this is NOT the case. If you don't show up for work you soon lose your job! Our school years also teach us how to deal with various personalities, make friendships, maintain friendships, deal with success and disappointment and grow as an individual as social demands and expectations grow. So when parents say 'oh he'll out grow it' or 'I was just like her and I turned out ok' you need to remember that not all children outgrow this desire to withdraw from the world and not all of them turn out 'ok'.

Tackling school refusal at its inception is the only way to avoid the consequences.

The short-term consequences of school refusal include:

- **Decline in academic performance.** The longer the child is absent from school the more learning and skill development they miss. If a child has had intermittent school refusal over several terms or perhaps years, then logically they have missed essential learning tasks that are built on and expanded in later years. Say, for example, that the child has missed several lessons on learning multiplication. When they eventually return to school they not only need to re-integrate but they also need to catch up. In a child who is already highly anxious about returning to school, this added pressure may be enough to push them out of school again or see them struggle to catch up.

- **Worsening peer relations.** It is a sad fact of life that the longer the child is absent the more likely their peer group will move on to new friendships. While teachers may do their best by sending 'warm fuzzies' (see Chapter 2) home to help the child feel appreciated and included the truth is that friends will eventually move on and find other children to play with. This makes a return to school awkward, embarrassing and lonely. The only way to stop this happening is to catch the nonattendance early hence eliminating the possibility of peer group shuffles.

- **Increasing family disharmony.** No matter how supportive parents can be, there comes a time when each parent will blame the other for the demise of their child. One parent may accuse the other of being 'too soft' while the other may be accused of being too harsh. The pressure of a parent having to be present to ensure that the child gets to school can also contribute to family disharmony and may result in frayed tempers. Siblings may also mimic behaviour to get out of school as we saw with Charles and his family. For many parents the dread of having to wake up to another fight to get their child to school can be overwhelming and produce extremely high levels of anxiety and stress which in turn compromises the parents' mental health.

- **Reduced self-esteem and self-confidence.** As the child disengages from daily activities that previously brought joy and fulfilment, so does their self-esteem (a favourable impression of oneself) and self-confidence (confidence in one's own judgement and ability) decline. They stop believing that they can achieve and become disempowered. Although they may say they are happiest at home they know this is not normal and therefore reinforces their negative image of self.

The long-term consequences of school refusal include:

- **Academic underachievement.** Academic under-achievement is defined as a discrepancy between a child's school performance and his or her actual ability. In the case of school refusers it is often not a lack of intelligence but rather a gap in learning that can lead to long-term academic underachievement. Once learning is stifled for extended periods of time it can be difficult to re-engage in alternative forms of education as the child enters adulthood. I have met many bright, insightful individuals who are in jobs that carry little enjoyment simply because they did not believe they had the intelligence or fortitude to do better. The only way to limit academic underachievement in this group is to catch the problem at its inception and limit the degree of lost learning.

- **Employment difficulties.** It is logical to presume that if a child or young person has missed large amounts of academic and life skills that employment difficulties will ensue. Having poor math, spelling and writing skills makes it difficult to obtain anything but the most rudimentary jobs which are often not secure and rarely well paid. There are exceptions to this but they are few and far between. Additionally, the chronic school refuser has often failed to learn the skills of resilience and endurance and may find going to work day in day out difficult, confronting and boring.

- **Low self-esteem.** Spending extended periods of time at home while peers are 'moving on with their lives' can reinforce feelings of worthlessness and helplessness. We can only imagine how hard it would be to hear about friends planning to go to university or travel or seek employment while you have been at home withdrawn from peers and life in general. It is difficult to develop good self-esteem when our actions are in stark contrast to our peers.

- **Poor peer relations.** Just because the school refuser grows into adulthood does not mean that they miraculously learn how to make and maintain friendships. On line friendships created through a shared interest in gaming or social websites are no substitute for the real thing. I can remember meeting a young man who informed me that he had in excess of 200 friends and was socially well connected but was unable to tell me when he'd last sat across a table from one of these 'friends' to share a meal, coffee or have a general discussion about every day life. On line friendships are a far cry from having to learn to compromise and adapt to fellow workers.

The following composite case example illustrates some of the issues discussed earlier in the chapter.

> Matthew was 15 years old when he came to my attention for school refusal and aggressive behaviour. His mother informed me that he had always liked school as a young child but had developed a real dislike for school as he got older and, in particular, since beginning high school. He was reported by teachers as a class clown who made bad choices when making friends, easily distracted in class and refusing to do homework, which had caused enormous problems at home. As his academic performance at primary school had always been on par with peers there had never been any suspicion that he may have had learning deficits. As Matthew got into more and more trouble at school, he began using any plausible excuse to get out of attending school. As his mother worked full-time, she was unable to enforce school attendance and would often only find out he'd missed school when she asked him directly. At the time of referral, Matthew was in Year 9 and had been disengaged from school for most of that year. He had attended school intermittently between Year 6 and Year 8.

> Upon assessment, Matthew was found to have learning deficits that would have made learning a challenge as he grew up and academic demands exceeded his ability. These deficits were also the likely cause of his behaviour in class and the friends he chose to be with. After much work with Matthew and his mother to address his anxiety about attending school and a significantly modified learning program put in place by his school, we were successful in getting Matthew back to school full-time.

> By this time, however, Matthew was well into Year 10 and struggling with his modified program. His friends had also moved on to new friendship groups leaving him feeling on the outer and awkward. After much discussion and deliberation, it was agreed that TAFE courses might be a better option but even these were found to be too challenging. The reality was that Matthew had missed a lot of learning and had lost faith in his ability to learn. Matthew left school at age 16 to seek employment.

I had no further contact with Matthew until he was 21 years old, when he returned for treatment of Depression. He reported long periods of unemployment and association with other unemployed youth who had introduced him to cannabis and a variety of other illicit drugs. Although he had managed to find some work during the five years since he'd left school, this work had often been for casual positions, which were short lived and poorly paid. Matthew had, at the time of referral, made a real effort to get his life back of track and had given up his drug use but in the process lost the only 'friends' he had. With no job and so much time on his hands Matthew found himself confined to his room, ruminating over his life and becoming more and more withdrawn from family. He was going to bed in the early hours of the morning and waking in the afternoon and only venturing out of his home if necessary. The combination of low self-esteem, poor education and limited social connectedness made Matthew a prime candidate for Depression.

Chapter 4

What professionals can do

Act promptly

I have been horrified to learn, while presenting this topic to parents, teachers and other professionals, that some schools do not intervene until the student's attendance drops below 30% to 35%! We need to recognise that by the time the student has taken this much time off school their school refusal is well and truly entrenched. If we are to curb this behaviour it must be investigated early. A system needs to be in place where absences of more than 2 to 3 days are immediately flagged as 'at risk' and investigated via telephone calls to parents. We need to remember that many parents leave for work long before their child leaves for school and may not even be aware, in the early stages, that their child is not attending school. I have come across a system in a few schools whereby any absenteeism without a phone call to explain the reason triggers a call to parents by an admin person. These systems are a brilliant way of keeping check on truancy and school refusal. There is no possibility of habits becoming ingrained as nonattendance is picked up on the day.

Once it is established that the child will be absent from school for more than a few days, it is crucial that the class teacher makes regular contact with the child and helps them feel like they are still part of the class by sharing news during their phone calls, sending home 'warm fuzzies' (short notes of encouragement and friendship) from each class mate and allowing the child to speak to friends. I was privileged to see the wonderful work of one teacher who enlisted the help of parents in her class and had one class friend per week visit my client in hospital and then at home. The class emissary would always carry notes and drawings from members of the class and, as the child became well enough, brought along small amounts of homework that the teacher would dutifully mark and return with the next emissary. These small interventions minimise the impact of the absence and encourage seamless re-engagement. Even when it is established that the child is well and refusing to attend school, it is crucial that every effort be made to maintain contact with the child and their family on a regular basis.

Establish cause

Once it is established that the child is absent for reasons other than medically proven ill health or family events, it is essential that all involved make it a priority to determine why the child has suddenly stopped attending school. The school counsellor or well being coordinator need to meet with the child, at school (a tacit first step at re-introduction), with and without parents to ascertain probable cause. Questioning could be centred around:

- Family function:

  - is a parent or sibling unwell

  - has a parent recently lost their job

  - has the family moved house recently

  - are parents arguing more than normal.

- Family history:

  - who else in the family has a history of anxiety or depression

- has anyone else in the immediate family had proble
  attending school.

- School:

  - classroom changes

  - friends absent

  - peer group shifts

  - bullying

  - impending activities that are disliked (i.e., school
    wimming program, exams, public speaking).

This is also an opportunity for discussion with specialist and
classroom teachers to determine if there have been any
changes in behaviour, social functioning, academic progress
and other shorter absences that were not picked up by the
early warning system.

The use of the School Refusal Assessment Scale — Revised
(SRAS-R; parent and child scale) could also be used to assist
in establishing cause. The SRAS-R identifies four functions
with the highest scoring function considered to be the
primary reason for school refusal.

Validate feelings and fears

Many of the children I see feel unheard by teachers and school
counsellors. I often hear them say that they have reported
their difficulties with schoolwork or the bullying in the playground and nothing has been done. I am aware that this is
often their perception and far from the truth but we must
remember that if the child does not feel that their feelings and
fears are validated they will be hesitant to engage in a return-
to-school program. Let them know that they have been heard
by repeating back to them what their fears and feelings are
and, if appropriate, write, in the form of a contract, the

)ol will take in order to ensure a successful
This could include an agreement that classes
extra help will be provided in subjects they
or allowances will be made for time out of
_.... wnen they feel overwhelmed.

Intervene quickly

If the child feels they have been heard and intervention begins immediately the likelihood of re-engagement is increased. If, for example, the child reports bullying in the playground and receives a phone call a day or two after disclosure and is told, in detail, the steps that have been taken to ensure this will not occur again, this action begins to reinstate the child's trust in their school and teachers. I remember a school that, on discovering that their school refuser was suffering with anxiety disorder, set up a safe zone where the child could retreat when they felt overwhelmed or stressed. The child could withdraw to this area by showing a small red card in class and was allowed a maximum of 20 minutes before they were expected to make an attempt to return to class. This student was encouraged to keep items they found soothing in this area to assist with their efforts to regain control of their anxiety.

Psychoeducation for the child

Psychoeducation is just a fancy way of saying 'teach the student as much as you can about their condition'. I always start by teaching my clients about anxiety. As we discussed in Chapter 1, it is essential that the student understands that the symptoms they experience are not life threatening and that, in fact, they are a normal part of life. For example, I always use the analogy of going on holidays to explain the anxiety the student feels when they attempt a return to school. When we prepare to go on holidays all focus is on our departure date.

We count down days, and then hours until we leave. While on holidays we are carefree and happy with few if any stresses to hinder us. As our holiday draws to an end we begin to re-engage with our lives back home by checking work emails, thinking about the things that need to be done before we can return to work and the workload we can expect upon our return. It is not uncommon to feel a little anxious the night before our return to work and we may even feel 'yuk' on the morning we return to work because, let's be honest, who really prefers work to holidays? I like to refer to this 'syndrome' as 'Post Holiday Blues'. Our level of anxiety about returning to work will be directly proportional to how much we like or dislike our job. In much the same way a return to school is directly proportional to how much the student likes or dislikes school. But, like it or not, we go back to work because we know we must. Just as the student needs to understand that returning to school is a must. I find that if the student can see that anxiety happens to grown-ups as well, they are better able to normalise/rationalise it in themselves.

The next step is to teach the student about school refusal as discussed in Chapter 2. This can be quite confronting for the student as it brings to light the reasons behind the disengagement. You'll often get hints of what is behind the refusal if you look closely at their reactions. Look for sudden fidgeting, inability to maintain eye contact, any attempts at redirection (i.e., asking for a drink, asking to go to the bathroom), angry outbursts or tears.

Psychoeducation for parents and teachers about school refusal and its treatment

Just as psychoeducation is essential for the student, so too is it important for parents and teachers. If a person feels knowledgeable, empowered and supported, their ability to cope with difficult situations grows exponentially. I find that once a parent knows that the return to school will be fraught with tears, tantrums and a variety of other symptoms, they are significantly less afraid when the time comes to be firm but fair. Similarly, teachers attending my workshops often express their feelings of helplessness when dealing with school refusal. This sense of 'not knowing what to do' can even extend beyond classroom teachers to include year level coordinators, vice principals, and principals.

Increasing the understanding of everyone involved about anxiety and how it relates to the problem helps the process of treatment. A visual representation approach to explain how anxiety levels relate to school refusal treatment (see Figure 4.1) has proved useful within my own work with parents and teachers.

The y axis in Figure 4.1 labelled 'Physiological Arousal' represents what we might call anxiety, stress, tension, nerves, and so on. Our body really does not care what we choose to call this arousal, it just knows that when we use these terms we have increased levels of cortisol (stress hormone) in our body that makes us feel like running or fighting. This is why the school refuser can become so aggressive or pose a flight risk when they are at their worst. This increase in physiological arousal is what makes us feel 'yuk' and brings on the symptoms of a panic attack that, in turn, make us reluctant to face whatever event brought on the panic symptoms. We associate those symptoms of panic with the event, in this case, attending school and we learn to avoid those feelings by avoiding school.

The long straight solid dark line on the graph represents the only people on earth who have zero anxiety/physiological arousal. When I ask a group I am working with to suggest who could possibly be free of anxiety all the time, the general responses are babies or the young. Even a baby, however, must cry in order to draw our attention to their hunger or dirty

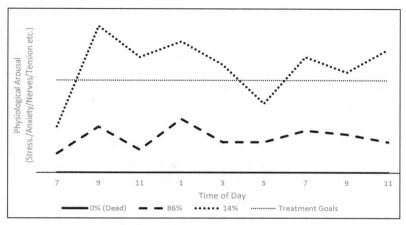

Figure 4.1 How anxiety levels relate to school refusal treatment

diaper. Very few respond with the correct answer — the dead. Yes, it is a trick question but I use it to emphasise that no-one lives without some level of anxiety or stress in their life and that as such they (the school refuser) cannot expect to go back to school without feeling some level of discomfort. Life produces stress and learning to live with it rather than hide from it is the only way to move forward.

The middle dashed line on the graph represents the 86% of humans who live with day-to-day levels of anxiety. Just like the clinical group (14%), they too experience peaks and troughs in their daily anxiety but the difference is that this group often work against the anxiety and challenge themselves to do those things that the 14% find impossible to do. Just like the clinical group, this group experience distress/anxiety/stress when they are caught in traffic on the way to work, argue with their partner or open the letterbox to several large bills. Unlike the clinical group, they do not allow this stress to take over. They may be distressed for a few minutes, hours and maybe even days but it does not define them. They move on and deal with the issue.

The top dotted line on the graph represents the 14% of the population who suffer clinical levels of anxiety. This group wakes up worrying. In the case of the school refuser they wake up worrying about going to school. The worry starts as soon as they reach consciousness resulting in their stress/anxiety levels rising steeply and rapidly. The school refuser gives these feelings of worry their undivided attention hence enabling stress/anxiety levels to rise even faster. If a parent is on their tail encouraging them to get ready for school the anxiety rises even more steeply resulting in a panic attack. We've already covered the symptoms of panic in Chapter 3, so we know that they can make you feel really 'blah' for quite some time, but having the panic attack also causes that physiological arousal to drop, which is why the school refuser feels so tired and sleepy after they've had one. As a parent it can be tempting to fall into the trap of letting them sleep it off for several hours and later agree that going to school 'this late' is probably not worth it.

The thin solid line on the graph represents the goal of treatment: to keep stress and anxiety *below* the line. In other words, if the student is taught, using a variety of strategies, to prevent the stress levels from getting too high then the chances of experiencing panic symptoms is significantly reduced and control is regained.

The x axis in Figure 4.1 is labelled 'Time of Day', which is divided into blocks of time that represent the average day. We can see that over time, if we intervene at regular intervals with our strategies, we stop arousal levels from becoming too high and therefore increase control. Likewise, if we use our strategies intermittently or rarely, our anxiety breaks through our efforts to control it and takes over.

Teach coping strategies

Once the student understands anxiety and school refusal it is time to teach coping strategies that will assist them in gaining control over the anxious symptoms they feel when preparing to go to school. Again, it is vital that the student understands that some level of discomfort is to be expected. I always point out that in my 30 years as a psychologist I've never met a school refuser who returns to school with no discomfort for the first few days and sometimes weeks. This helps to normalise the anxiety and when it appears does not cause panic and fear. Treatment strategies for school refusers are provided in Chapter 6. Chapters 7 and 8 provide more specific treatment strategies for high achievers, and students with ASD, respectively.

Enlist parental support

As we have previously discussed, parental support is essential if we are to be successful in returning a student to full-time schooling. We can have our best teachers, school counsellors, case workers, youth workers and anyone else who can be involved, but if the student's parents are not on board with our approach, all is lost. Parents are our front line people. They are the ones who emotionally and physically prepare the student for school. If they weaken to the pleas and tears of the student, all the great work put in by teachers, psychologists, and others involved falls flat.

I have found the best way to enlist parental support is to explain to them that they are our 'co-therapists'. We teach them so that they can teach and support their child. In any given interaction with a family, I will spend at least 3 to 4 sessions (intermittently) with the primary care giver to get them up to speed and educate them as to what they can expect and how things are likely to progress. I find, just like the student, that if parents understand what is happening, how it happens and what they can do to help, we very quickly have them on board. It is essential that once we have parental support that they are supported throughout the return to school.

Involve support services

Sometimes parents are so frazzled by their attempts at getting their child to school that they simply have nothing left to give or have their own issues that make commitment to getting their child back to school impossible. These are the families that may benefit from the involvement of support services such as those provided by the Victorian State Government (the Child FIRST referral and support service, and the Navigator program), which actively seek to re-engage children and young adults in education.

Where necessary, referral to the relevant state or territory human services department may also be appropriate to ensure that the student is given the best chance of returning to school.

Using a return to school plan

Once all the aforementioned steps have been taken the time then comes for a return-to-school plan to be established and signed by all parties. This plan can be as slow as it needs to be but there is no room for going back. I always encourage small manageable steps that have the greatest possibility of success. The return-to-school plan needs to have clear rewards for attendance and consequences for nonattendance. If the parents or student have any doubts about the origins of the symptoms exhibited a thorough examination by a general practitioner or specialist needs to be undertaken so that fears can be dispelled BEFORE we begin a return to school.

A example of what a return-to-school plan might look like is shown in Figure 4.2.

DAY	GOAL	REWARD	CONSEQUENCE
Monday	Arrive at school by 9.15. Sit in library reading a book until 10.15 am.	30 mins on iPad	No electronics; 2 additional chores
Tuesday	Arrive school 9am. Sit in library reading book until 10.15 am.	35 mins on iPad	No electronics; 2 additional chores
Wednesday	Arrive school 9am. Sit in library reading book until 10.30 am.	40 mins on iPad	No electronics; 2 additional chores
Thursday	Arrive school 9 am. Sit in library until recess then leave library with friend for 10 mins in playground either mixing with other children or walking around.	50 mins on i-Pad and 10 mins towards staying up late on Friday or Saturday night.	No electronics; 2 additional chores
Friday	Arrive 9am. Library until recess. Stay outside with friend until the end of recess	55 mins on i-Pad and another 10 mins towards staying up late on Friday or Saturday night.	No electronics; 2 additional chores

Figure 4.2 Example return-to-school plan

The aim of the plan is to provide structure and direction in a manner in which the student is most likely to succeed IF they are actively using their newly taught strategies. Where the student claims they cannot succeed we need to consider two things:

1. Is the student genuinely anxious and wanting to get better or are they using their anxiety to justify their ongoing absences? There is no doubt that some students, often older students, may have genuine causes for the onset of their school refusal but then become accustomed to the simpler and less stressful life of being at home and use their anxiety as a means to an end. This is the group who will often refuse to help themselves and may exhibit self-injurious behaviour and talk

of suicide to ensure that parents and teachers become afraid and offer no further challenge.

While all threats of self-harm should be investigated by a doctor, psychiatrist or psychologist, we must keep in mind that sometimes a threat to their own life is the only way these students have succeeded in the past to remove the threat of re-engagement. For example, I met a 16-year-old girl in Year 11, who had missed school intermittently throughout Year 9 and Year 10 but had failed to attend most of Year 11. When previous attempts had been made to get her back to school, she would talk about hating herself and wishing she was dead, which automatically caused her mother to scale down attempts to get her back to school. The student admitted, several months into treatment, that she knew she frightened her mother with her talk of self-harm and death and that she used this strategy as her 'trump card' to avoid returning to school.

2.   If the student appears to try but is overwhelmed by their anxiety then a referral to a child/adolescent psychiatrist for medication may be timely.

The return-to-school plan should, on a daily basis, reintroduce a small part of school expectations. For example, the student can start by reading a book in the library for the first few days but is then introduced to small, manageable amounts of schoolwork. Then the expectation would be that they begin to mingle with other students at recess and lunchtime. The pressure of this step could be reduced by a friend calling into the library and going into the playground with the student. We would then expect that the student begin attending classes even if it is at the rate of one lesson in class and the next in the library.

The thing to keep in mind is that the longer we stay on each step the more likely it is that anxiety will escalate when the next phase is introduced. Keeping the goals small and changing will help keep the anxiety manageable as the student has no time to become accustomed to that step. This is one of the reasons why weekends can be a real drainer for parents because their child has two days to get comfortable and 'forget' what is expected of them from Monday to Friday.

One of the biggest challenges when returning a student to school is providing parents, teachers and the student with proof of their improvements, no matter how small they may be. The Subjective Units of Distress Scale (SUDS) can be useful in achieving this goal (see Figure 4.3). SUDS can be measured in the form of a thermometer where zero represents no anxiety while five represents extreme anxiety. Each escalation in anxiety carries with it a suggested intervention. For example:

- a little anxious carries the suggestion: find something different to do (distraction)

- feeling uncomfortable: start breathing exercises, tissue blowing, bubble blowing

- difficulty thinking clearly: breathing exercises plus distraction

- mind racing, clammy hands: remove yourself from the environment and go for a brisk walk, get a drink, sing to myself.

- racing mind, difficulty breathing, pounding heart: withdraw to a safe area where you can engage in relaxation and/or mindfulness practices, use an over the counter remedy that may help, use your stress ball.

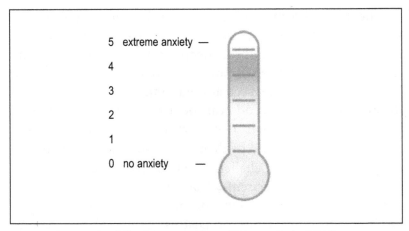

Figure 4.3 Example of The Subjective Units of Distress Scale (SUDS)

Each SUDS can be tailored to suit the student's needs and incorporate strategies that they know will work. In addition to being a quick reference on what to do at different anxiety levels, it is also an excellent way for the student to see their SUDS drop as they implement strategies. Similarly teachers and parents can use SUDS to remind the student of their appropriate strategies while also seeing for themselves the gradual reduction in anxiety as the student gains more and more control. I often suggest that the SUDS be printed onto A4 paper and laminated. They can then be placed around the house, in lockers or in diaries for easy reference.

It can be useful for parents/teachers to note their subjective evaluation of a student's anxiety at various times in the day and then present these to the student after Day 2 or Day 3 of re-engagement as a way of proving that their efforts are paying off. For example, on Day 1 of re-engagement, the parent may rate the students SUDS at 5/5 as they walk from the house to the car to be taken to school but then on Day 2 SUDS may be rated at 4/5 or 3/5.

Home schooling/distance education

It is a legal requirement in Australia that every school-age child attend school and parents can be fined for failing to ensure attendance. There are, howver, two accepted alternatives. Professionals working in the area of school refusal will sometimes come across the issues of *home schooling* and *distance education* as alternatives to conventional schooling. This is an area not always immediately well understood by non teachers but is important for other professionals to understand.

Home schooling

This type of schooling is where parents assume overall responsibility for the planning, implementation and assessment of their child's education. Depending on which state you live in, the government will legislate a number of key learning areas that need to be incorporated into any home schooling program as well as systems to ensure its correct use. While home schooling might initially be appealing to parents you need to consider whether they have the time to implement all the demands of home schooling and whether they have the stamina and resilience to keep their child motivated and on task.

Distance Education

This type of schooling is where the student is not physically in a classroom but has the same curriculum as other students of their age. Teaching and learning programs can be completed on line, via disk or in print. Contact methods with teachers include phone, e-mail, chat, bulletins or mail. Although distance education can provide quality education to the motivated student, my experience suggests that it can fall short for those students who have had long periods away from school and lack the discipline and motivation to stay focused and on task.

Often when parents and schools agree that all attempts at re-engagement have failed home schooling or distance education can be an option. Home schooling or distance education can work very well in cases where a student has become unwell and recovery will take several months, where the family moves to remote areas where schools are many kilometres from home, or where families travel for extended periods but want their student to stay abreast of their education. Even in these valid cases, however, we need to be aware of the dangers of the social isolation and relationship deficits that can arise from being removed from mainstream schooling. Home schooled/distance education students miss out on learning how to work cooperatively with others, how to make and keep friends who do not exist in cyberspace, lack the input of others in what is being taught and the routines of attending school daily that are the precursors to building the stamina and resilience required to becoming a full-time worker in adulthood.

While I understand that these programs resolve the issue of the student's anxiety and school attendance in the short term, they also delay the inevitable. At some point, the student and their family will have to address the anxiety and learn to manage it effectively. The longer the period away from school, the greater the anxiety to re-engage not only with school and friends but with their wider community as well. I have dealt with several families who have taken these options (mainly distance education) and upon follow up discovered that the student is disengaged from all education and unemployed.

I understand that schools have a legal obligation to provide families with options if they cannot get their child to school but distance education and home schooling must be THE LAST resort. These options may facilitate eventual school disengagement due to the loss of daily accountability and structure.

If distance education becomes the 'last resort' then it is essential that parents and teachers stay vigilant in maintaining the student's engagement and establishing regular social interactions whether they be of an academic or sporting nature.

Chapter 5

What parents can do

Whether we like it or not, when we become parents we not only take on the responsibility of raising our young by providing them with food and shelter but also their emotional and psychological well being. When it comes to school refusal, it is the parents who lead the way and **show** their child, in words and action, that they not only **believe** the child can return to school but that they, as parents, have the strength and resilience to see the child through this difficult time.

Children, irrespective of age, have an uncanny ability to sense a parent's distress or doubt. Think of all the times you have had a rough day and your child comes home and asks, without prompt, 'what's wrong?'. In younger children their sensing that something is wrong may translate to clingy or sullen behaviour. While in adolescents it may be a flat out 'what's up with you?'. The fact is, we can't fool our children. Their biological connection to us, and their intuitive nature, will help them spot our doubt. This is why it is essential that the child senses that there is no doubt on your behalf. **Believe** that your child can return to school and tell them so. Don't let them see you worry. Present a confident, strong, supportive persona and you will present yourself to your child as someone who does not doubt for a moment that they will get back to school. This is why it is crucial for parental anxiety and distress to be addressed BEFORE we attempt a return to school. Where possible, I have parents attend skills development sessions with their child so that parents are experienced in using mindfulness and relaxation practices and can use them before, during, and after dealing with their school refuser. Let's look at an example of how this might play out:

> You wake up in the morning already feeling sick to the stomach about having to get your school refuser to school. Before you go in to wake them, you take a few deep breaths, clear your mind and put on a happy, confident face. You walk to their bedroom and begin the process of waking them. You keep doing your breathing exercises and keep your thoughts calm. You reiterate as many times as required that today is a school day and they WILL be going to school. In the face of tears, screaming, swearing, or outright defiance, you stay strong and continue saying to yourself, 'If I give in now all my efforts will have been for nothing'. If need be, you return to your own room, calm yourself and go out for round two! Use your breathing exercises, mantras, stress balls or whatever else you find calming but (as my favourite poem says) 'never, ever give up because the prize is often close at hand'.

Listening and validating your child's fears and feelings about school is important because we want the child to feel that they do not need to hide the real reason(s) for not wanting to attend school. If parents minimise or belittle how the child feels, the child is more likely to believe that the parents don't care and that they must face the issue alone.

There are times when being a parent means you are busy all day, every day. When a child stops attending school we need to MAKE TIME to contact their school and speak to their class teacher or year level coordinator to determine what has brought about the child's need to avoid school. As discussed in Chapter 2, the reasons for children not wanting to attend school are as varied and complex as any child can be. Parents cannot expect the school to 'fix the problem' because while the issue of nonattendance may have originated at school, it is played out in the home and sometimes its reoccurrence comes from the inconsistencies in the home environment more so than what is occurring at school.

Here are some practical tips parents might find useful when dealing with school refusal:

- In younger children, reassure your child that you will be back to pick them up at the end of the school day. Be on time but avoid waiting at the classroom door, which builds the expectation that **you** will wait for them. Instead, teach your child to play on the playground equipment immediately after school and to wait for you there. This will provide a distraction for your child, and there will be no expectation that you will be at their classroom door as soon as they exit. This tactic allows for those occasions when you are stuck in traffic or held up at work. If they are accustomed to playing with others on the playground equipment for a few minutes every day, a short delay will not be noticed and anxiety will be held at bay.

- For those occasions when being late cannot be helped, it is crucial that the child has a well rehearsed back-up plan. You could, for example, teach your child that if lots of children have left the playground area that they are to make their way back to the classroom or the front office so that you can be called. If the child knows in advance what to do, their anxiety is less likely to escalate. These strategies not only give parents breathing time for school pick-ups but it aids in the development of independence and resilience in the child, making it a win–win situation.

- Children often long to be at home with parents doing fun things. For this reason it is important that parents not give detailed information of the things they will be doing while the child is at school. Knowing, for example, that you will be having lunch with 'grandma' will not foster positive feelings towards school. If asked, always make your day sound boring.

- Try to avoid school goodbyes. If your child is already anxious about being at school, long and drawn out goodbyes will only make their anxiety worse. If you feel the need to walk your child to class, be sure to keep the goodbyes short and positive (e.g., say something like, 'Oh look there's your friend. You have a good day and I'll see you this afternoon out by the playground area. Bye'). At this point you walk away; no looking back; no further discussion. Remember, the more anxious you sound or look, the more your child will mirror your distress. Ideally, to avoid long goodbyes, the child could be dropped off at the 'drop-off zone' and encouraged to walk to class alone or if you genuinely feel that you cannot drop and go then have your child brought to school by a parent whose child is your child's friend. This eliminates long goodbyes and develops friendships and self-esteem.

- Younger and older students alike may find it useful and calming to arrive at school a little earlier, and assist a favourite teacher set up for the day. This provides distraction while the parent leaves, and purpose as they are doing something to assist. It also builds self-esteem because they feel their efforts are valued.

- When your school refuser begins crying, or looks sick, or rants and raves, it is essential that they be reminded that they have been taught strategies to aid with their anxiety and that it is their responsibility to use them. If need be, you can assist by sitting with them and helping regain control of their breathing or calm their crying, but at no point do you give in and allow them to stay home or come back home if you've managed to get them as far as school. We must remember that EVERY time a parent gives in to the tears, pleas and tantrums we make the behaviour more ingrained and we teach the child that if they cry, plead or have tantrums long enough and hard enough, we will eventually give in.

• If you are called to your child's school to take them home, you should request that the child be placed in 'sick bay' and where possible have a school counsellor, school nurse or well being coordinator assist them in using their strategies to return to a calm state. If need be, and you must attend the school, sit in sick bay with your child and run through their coping strategies until they regain control. Unless it is absolutely necessary, you should not take your child home. The aim must always be to return the child to the classroom or wherever their return-to-school program requires them to be. By remaining at school and NOT taking the child home we are teaching them that they are capable of regaining control, which builds self-esteem and resilience.

Using rewards and consequences

As previously discussed, it is up to parents (with the aid of a school counsellor or psychologist) to establish clear rewards for staying at school and firm and consistent consequences for not attending school. If, for example, the return-to-school plan requires the child to be at school for two hours in order to be rewarded with 30 minutes on their iPad, we cannot acquiesce because they attended for 30 minutes or an hour. They may, perhaps, have 7 minutes or 15 minutes but 30 minutes on their iPad is only granted when two hours are completed at school. Suggestions for rewards and consequences could include:

- Rewards:

  - more Internet time

  - later bed times (an extra 15 minutes each day they are at school to be used on a Friday or Saturday night)

  - outings with friends (play dates for younger children, movies or shopping trips with older children).

  - special time with parents (i.e., coffee dates, bike riding, fishing, cooking together)

  - special treats in lunch boxes (treats that are not often allowed)

  - money (a last resort and only in amounts that are affordable. In younger children this needs to be dispensed at the end of each day as weekly can seem like a lifetime away and they lose interest)

  - a favourite toy or game that is earned in the form of tokens or piece by piece (i.e., LEGO^{TM}).

- Consequences:

  - Disabling or removing electronics from the house before parents go to work (including TV remotes)

  - several chores to be completed by day's end (preferably chores they dislike)

  - refusal to drive the child around (particularly good for older children)

  - refusal to take them for driving lessons

  - disconnecting mobile phone services

  - withholding pocket money

  - removing luxury items from their bedroom.

In order for rewards to have the desired effect, it is essential that they be earned ONLY when the student has achieved their individual return to school goal. In other words, it is of little value if you are offering more iPad time but the student has access to electronic devices on demand. As in the real world, rewards are earned and not a right, therefore, access to the Internet or electronics is earned just as we, as adults, earn our pay or bonuses at work.

Ultimately, our role as parents is to produce happy, resilient and functioning members of society. Sometimes this means having to be **firm** but at all times **fair**. Belittling, condemning or refusing to praise or reward effort is simply not on. When I work with families and their school refuser to establish return-to-school plans I always emphasise the benefits and rewards. I explain that the introduction of consequences is completely in their hands and that no-one involved is actually interested in dispensing consequences, it benefits everyone if rewards are earned. If the currency (rewards) is right, change **will** happen.

Finally, as parents, we have to ask ourselves what kind of role model are we? I know this can be confronting but ask yourself if how you live imparts the right messages to your children? Are you up in the morning, showered and ready to start your day? Do your children see you achieving tasks? Do they see you confront difficult situations with maturity and resilience? If not then perhaps the time has come to seek some help for yourself. There is no shame is asking for help and there are many services that can assist. Perhaps start by speaking to your local GP who will begin the referral process.

Chapter 6

Treatment for school refusal

The aim of treatment for school refusal is to provide the child with strategies that allow control of anxiety symptoms hence enabling attendance at school without high levels of distress.

Teaching children strategies they can use throughout the school day not only aids in the management of anxiety but also ensures that their thinking remains rational. When the body is tense and stressed the brain releases cortisol (the stress hormone) to fight the perceived threat that our stressed body suggests. The more cortisol, the more anxious we feel, the more anxious we feel the less likely we are to think logically and clearly and regain control. Indeed, the more anxious we become the 'dumber' we get because our body is geared for fight or flight, not logical thought and action. Our prefrontal cortex, the part that does the higher order thinking, goes off line when cortisol is released. The cool thing is, though, that every time we engage in one of the techniques to follow we help relax our body, which encourages the brain to release the antidote to cortisol. We actually have the antidote all geared up and ready for release and it's called oxytocin. Oxytocin is known as the love hormone but also has a calming and soothing effect, which is exactly what you want when you're feeling stressed and wound up. The half-life of oxytocin, however, is less than that of cortisol, which is why we need to keep our efforts up when we're trying to maintain control of anxiety through the strategies outlined in this chapter. It is recommended that children use these strategies on an hourly or two hourly basis beginning as soon as they wake in the morning to the minute they go to bed at night. The use of an alarm, notification on a smartphone or the sounding of the school bell can be used as a prompt to remind the child to undertake whatever strategies they prefer.

Mindfulness and relaxation

Breathing exercises

One of the most powerful techniques that can be taught to the school refuser (or indeed, the anxious parent[s]) is the effective use of breath. Breathing exercises are simple but highly effective and underlie most other techniques. Although we all breathe, not all of us do so effectively when we are distressed. When we become distressed, our breathing becomes short and shallow. This short, shallow breathing is sufficient to keep us from fainting but not enough to relax the muscles. If our breathing is deep, slow and rhythmical, our red blood cells carry that oxygen to all parts of our body and cause the muscles to relax. If muscles are relaxed then there is no message travelling from the body to the brain to request that cortisol be released to fight the perceived threat. If no cortisol is released there is no fight or flight response and if there is no fight or flight response then there is no anxiety. I always teach my clients to practise breathing exercises regularly and to aim for approximately 10 breaths every time they hear their phone alarm or school bell go off. The beauty of breathing exercises is that they can be done anywhere, any time with no-one being the wiser. They can be done in the car on the way to school, during class, on the way to your locker or in the canteen line. This is how I teach breathing exercises — on hearing the school bell or phone alarm:

- drop your shoulders
- stand or sit up straight

- draw in a long, slow, deep breath
- hold it for just one second
- slowly let it out
- do not repeat until that first breath is completely gone
- repeat.

There are many variations to teaching breathing exercises but I have found this technique to be very effective. I have come across many books that suggest breathing in to the count of 4 and then breath out for the count of 4 but this method requires that attention be drawn away from the events going on at that time in order to engage in the breathing exercise. My variation allows the person to continue with day-to-day activities as there is no counting or need to remove oneself from their immediate environment. Unlike many books on anxiety that espouse the virtues of breathing exercises and suggest that they be used when panic symptoms begin I suggest that they be used to PREVENT panic symptoms by using them at regular intervals throughout the day whether it is deemed a good or bad day. This technique is a 'no-brainer'. You just need to remember to breathe deeper and slower than you normally do.

Breathing exercises are very effective but they can get a bit boring if you are a little person, so here are a few variations that may be more effective with younger children:

- **Tissue blowing.** Take a tissue and separate the two layers so that you end up with two very thin tissues. Take one of these tissues and throw it up into the air. The challenge is to keep the tissue up in the air as long as possible. Keep count of how long the child can keep it up in the air and challenge them to better their previous effort. This technique has a two-pronged benefit because it helps the child refocus and increases oxygen intake. It's also loads of fun to do in a classroom setting as it inevitably leads to people bumping into one another and everyone laughing. What a wonderful way to release tension and bring about class cohesion!

- **Bubbles.** Take a big glass of water and put a drop or two of dishwashing liquid into it. If you like, you can add a drop of food colouring as well. Place the glass into a big bowl, pop a straw into the glass and have the child blow bubbles. The challenge is to make so many bubbles that they overflow from the glass and into the bowl. This is a wonderful and fun way of increasing oxygen, reducing anxiety and redirecting attention.

The one minute relax

The one minute relax is a simple but effective technique that combines breathing exercises and mindfulness practices in a short period. This technique is ideal for the school refuser to undertake while visiting the bathroom at school, or in the car on the way to school or for the parent who is gearing up for the morning challenge of getting their child to school. To practise the one minute relax:

- Find yourself a quiet place to sit.
- Sit with a straight back and your head looking straight ahead.
- Turn your palms up on your lap (this makes your shoulders drop), and have your feet flat on the ground.
- Now slowly close your eyes and start concentrating on the air going in your nose, through the air passages and down into your lungs. You might like to imagine that the air is coloured so that you can more easily imagine

it spreading right down to the bottom of your lungs and then back out again. If your mind wanders (this will happen A LOT when you first start, so persevere), bring it back to the breathing.

- Keep your breathing slow, deep and rhythmical; continue for approximately one minute.

- Slowly open your eyes have a stretch or shake yourself out and you are done.

Hand on the heart

The hand-on-heart technique[1] is a centring technique that assists with refocusing and de-stressing. The only downside of this technique is that it cannot be done anywhere, at anytime. It is more for the morning before school, between lessons, while the student is in their quiet area, as they get home from school or before bed. Like all mindfulness and relaxation techniques, hand on the heart calms the body and mind therefore allowing the brain to release the oxytocin. To practise this breathing technique:

- Find a quiet place, and sit with your feet flat on the ground and your back straight.

- Using your dominant hand feel around on your chest until you can hear your heartbeat. It may be faint so pay attention.

- Once you've found your heartbeat, close your eyes and focus completely on your heartbeat; notice the depth, tone, sound; notice if there's any difference between the beats; notice how it feels inside your chest.

- If your mind wanders bring it back to the heartbeat and throughout the exercise keep your breathing deep and rhythmical. Do this for 2 to 3 minutes to start with and increase to 5–10 minutes as you become better at staying focussed.

This is a powerful technique so it does not take long for its calming and refocusing power to be felt.

Riverbank[2]

The riverbank technique is a great one for when you cannot shut down the chatter in your head (or what my yoga teacher calls 'the monkey mind'). This technique is especially good at night when you or your child get into bed and your first thoughts are of the struggles that you anticipate for the next day. To practise the riverbank technique:

- Find yourself a comfortable position in bed.

- Close your eyes and take a long, slow deep breath.

- Let the breath out slowly.

- Imagine yourself sitting on a riverbank. The sun is warm and soothing, the grass beneath you is soft and comfortable. As you look into the flowing waters of the river you realise that the river has the ability to renew and cleanse itself constantly. You notice how a leaf that falls into the water is washed away out of eyesight, down the river and eventually out to sea. In fact, anything that falls or is thrown into the water is simply washed away. I want you to throw EVERY SINGLE THOUGHT you have into the flowing waters of the river and I want you to watch them float out of sight.

- To make the connection between your inner and outer world stronger, I want you to tap your index finger, against your body or the mattress, each time you throw a thought into the water.

- Make sure that ALL thoughts are thrown into the river. By tapping out the thoughts you'll notice that initially the thoughts that are thrown into the river come thick and fast but as your brain registers that you're no longer paying attention to what the thoughts are the brain begins to slow down and the thoughts begin to come slower and slower. That's the funny thing with thoughts, when we don't pay attention to them and just let them flow into consciousness and then back out again without analysis or judgement, they fade and disappear.

- If you find yourself getting caught up in the thought just bring your attention back to throwing it in the river and watch it float away.

Once you get the hang of this technique it becomes easier to silence the 'monkey mind' and sleep comes so much quicker.

Mantras

The use of mantras is steeped in Hinduism and Buddhism. A mantra is a word, phrase or sound that is repeated to aid concentration in meditation. Mantras tend to be short and concise making them easy to remember. The repetition of a mantra is believed to affirm its meaning to ourselves and aid us in changing our thought processes. In the case of the school refuser, some helpful mantras might include:

- I can do this.

- It's just anxiety it cannot harm me.

- Stay positive.

- I am calm.

- I am prepared.

- Every day will be easier.
- I am stronger than I think.
- I will succeed.
- I will not give in.

Mandalas

Mandalas (see Figure 6.1) have been around for decades but have made a resurgence over the past few years as 'adult colouring' to promote mindfulness and relaxation. Mandalas are a wonderful way of redirecting attention, calming the breath and relaxing the mind and body. The more detailed the mandala, the greater the concentration. I often encourage families to have mandala books and colouring pencils in the car for the ride to and from school. Mandalas also work well in quiet rooms as they provide quick recovery from heightened anxiety and the student will have created a beautiful artwork worth framing. There are hundreds of mandalas for children and adults available on the Internet, so cost is not a factor.

FIGURE 6.1 Example mandala outline

Exercise

We all know the benefits of exercise and this is no less true in the school refuser. All too often children and adults spend too much time interacting with screens and not enough time getting the exercise that the mind and body require in order to function optimally. When we exercise, our bodies release chemicals called endorphins. Endorphins trigger positive feelings in the body that help us feel clear headed, happy and energetic. Wherever possible the school refuser should be encouraged to walk to and from school, with or without a support person, and they should be encouraged to engage in physical activity on a regular basis. Dancing classes, football clinics, soccer, cricket are all great ways of getting children and young adults out from behind their screens and into the real world. Even when anxiety begins to rise at school a brisk walk around the oval, while under the watchful eye of a teacher, may be all that is required to bring about a sense of calm.

Progressive muscle relaxation

Progressive muscle relaxation is a great way to release tension stored in the body and can be used in any environment where the person can be alone and in a relatively quiet room. To practise this technique:

- Sit with your feet flat on the floor, straight back and head looking straight ahead.

- Close your eyes and focus on your breathing being deep, slow and rhythmical.

- Tense all the muscles in your feet, hold for the count of five and release.

- Tense your calf muscles, hold for the count of five and release.

- Tense your thighs, hold for the count of five and release.

- Suck your tummy in (imagine that your belly button can touch your spine), hold for the count of five and release.

  Take in a deep breath (imagine that the air is reaching your belly button), hold for the count of five and release.

- Scrunch your shoulders up to your ears, hold for the count of five and release.

- Scrunch your shoulder blades together, hold for the count of five and release.

- Make a fist with your right hand, squeeze really hard tensing all the muscles in the hand and arm, hold for the count of five and release.

- Make a fist with your left hand, squeeze really hard tensing all the muscles in the hand and arm, hold for the count of five and release.

- Clench your teeth together, hold for the count of five and release.

- Scrunch up your face, hold for the count of five and release.

- Gently tilt your head towards your right shoulder, hold for the count of five and release.

- Gently tilt your head towards the left shoulder, hold for the count of five and release.

- Drop your chin to your chest, hold for the count of five and release.

- Tilt your head back towards your spine, hold for the count of five and release.

- Now using your mind's eye search through your body, gather up any remaining stress or tension, and blow it out with one big breath.

- Return to focusing on your deep, slow rhythmical breathing for a minute or two then slowly open your eyes and have a big stretch.

Centring exercises

When everything feels like it's spinning out of control helping the student regain control is our primary objective. Centring exercises are a great way of doing this and can be done in a formal or informal way. Each step of the exercise should only take a minute or two so it should only take a few minutes to complete.

- **Hearing.** Have the student sit with their eyes closed (or open but fixated on an object or point in the room) and ask them to focus on what they can hear in the room. For example, I can hear the ticking of the clock, the sound of you (the parent or teacher) moving in your chair, the air-conditioner working, the walls creaking. Now have the student focus on what they can hear outside the room. For example, I can hear birds singing, the wind, students walking outside. Now have the student focus on sounds that are much further away; those that they need to strain to hear. For example, I can hear traffic on the highway, a plane overhead, a truck reversing. Now have the student focus on the sounds outside the room, then back to themselves and finally have them open their eyes.

Without fail, this technique will help to centre the student and lower anxiety.

- **Touch.** Have the student choose a textured object. It can be fluffy, rough or spikey. If you are at home, the family pet is a great idea. Have the student close their eyes and have them focus first on how they are feeling (i.e., tired, annoyed, shortness of breath) then stroke the pet or object. Ask what it feels like to be touching the object. For example, ask them, 'Is it soft and warm?'; 'Is it abrasive on the skin?'. Then ask them to focus on the object or pet. Ask them 'Is the fabric on the soft toy the same all over?' If not, 'What is the difference?'; 'What part of the dog are you touching?'; 'Can you feel it breathe?' Once you have spent a few minutes focusing on the toy or pet, return to how the student is feeling now.

- **Unstructured.** Have the student become aware of what is outside the window of the classroom. "Who can you see playing outside? Which teachers do you see out on yard duty? What sort of day is it? Is it windy? What do you think those two students might be talking about?" This works just as effectively in the car on the way to school. You can either draw the child's attention to what is happening outside or you can turn it into a game and have them accumulate points for every white car they see. Once they've been playing for a few minutes ask them to check in with themselves to notice the improvements. If they say they feel no different point out the improvements you see; for example, you might say 'Your breathing is back to normal'; 'You're not wringing your hands anymore'.

Cognitive-Behaviour Therapy (CBT)

Cognitive–behaviour therapy (CBT) works from the premise that the way a person perceives a situation is more closely related to their reaction to the situation than the situation itself. In the case of the school refuser, they perceive attending school as a negative and stressful event based on past events that, in turn, makes it difficult for them to see the fun side of school: learning, sharing, making friends. CBT aims to change the person's unhelpful thinking and behaviour by utilising techniques that improve overall mood and function.

A simple way to explain the thought process that CBT addresses is provided in Figure 6.2. The way we think directly impacts on the way we feel that, in turn, influences the way we behave and the way we behave directly affects the way we think.

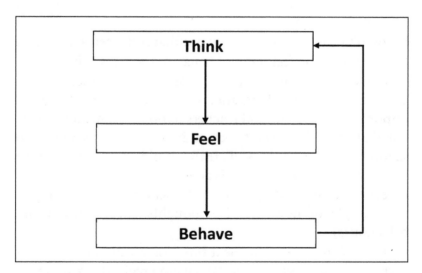

Figure 6.2 The thought process behind CBT.

If we apply this to the school refuser it looks like this:

> I wake up thinking about how much I hate going to school and instantly start to feel anxious about having to get up. At first I feel sick in the stomach and feel hot and cold but that's replaced by anger when mum comes in and tells me to get ready. I lash out at her and tell her to get out, throwing my pillow at her when she doesn't do it immediately. I start to cry, partially because I'm angry, but more so because I'm scared that she's going to make me go. As I alternate between being angry and scared I realise that I really, really hate school and that I'm definitely NOT going.

Variations on this scenario are played out every day with school refusers but imagine what would happen if we could change the thinking component. If the student could wake up thinking:

> I really don't want to go to school but I know I have to and I know that anything that takes a person out of their comfort zone is going to make them feel bad. This will be easier tomorrow and easier again the day after that. I just need to bite the bullet and do the exercises I've been taught. They WILL help. I just have to stay positive. Plus if I stay home I'll have no electronics and mum will leave me with a tonne of chores to complete so I might as well go.

It doesn't take a genius to work out that if the self-talk can be changed then the feelings and behaviour will also change.

While it is important for the school refuser to learn more about how their thinking affects their behaviour it is just as important for parents and teachers to do the same. It is essential that these important players in the student's return to school understand how THEIR thinking and behaviour impacts the student. I find this activity assists with insight and reflection for students, parents and teachers (see Figure 6.3 for an example of how negative thoughts affect feelings and behaviours).

The task is simple. The next time you are about to interact with the student ask yourself: 'What am I really thinking about my child or this student?'. If, as the example in Figure 6.3 suggests, it is negative and shrouded in doubt, you can be assured that the child or student will pick up on this and use

THINK	FEEL	BEHAVE
Oh no tomorrow's Monday	Sad	timidly
I can't be bothered	Angry	aggressively
Why can't she be normal	Deflated	flustered
This is hopeless	defeated	flat, directionless
How hard should I push	scared	hesitant

Figure 6.3 Example of how negative thoughts affect feelings and behaviours..

it to avoid going to school. It is important that we ask ourselves what we can do to change our presentation.

Behavioural activation

Behavioural activation is a fancy way of saying 'start changing the way you've been doing things and DO it differently'. Often when students have been at home for extended periods they develop unhelpful habits that perpetuate the problem. For example, a student who has not been to school for many weeks or months may begin going to bed later and later, which impacts on their ability to get up in time for school. To change this we begin winding back bedtime to a more reasonable time. This may include the confiscation of all electronics two hours before bedtime so that the mind can begin to wind down and facilitate a more natural sleep. If the student spends all day, every day, indoors playing computer games or watching TV we would aim to start getting them out of the house on a daily basis to engage in a brisk walk, run or bike ride.

Clear boundaries

The setting of clear boundaries is an important part of returning your student to school and an important part of any CBT program. By setting clear boundaries we eliminate 'grey areas'. Clear boundaries might include stating; for example:

- 'Unless you wake up with a high temperature, a cold is not an excuse for missing school', or 'getting your period does not entitle you to a day or two off school'. Any time off school for 'serious illness' will need to be confirmed by a doctor and will be spent in bed without electronics. While unwell, bedtime will be one hour earlier to assist with a speedy recovery.

- 'In preparation for your return to school you will be expected to wake up no later than 8 am and engage in some form of physical activity for a minimum of 30 minutes before 10 am'.

- 'You are expected to shower before midday and complete all chores before engaging in any other activity'.

- 'You have chosen to drop out of school. That is your decision given that you are 17 but if you do not have a job within four weeks you will be expected to engage in some form of volunteering on a daily basis. When not at your volunteer work you will take on the duties previously completed by your mother/father, including, but not limited to, clothes washing, cooking, general house cleaning and pet care'.

While these may seem blunt, they leave no room for argument and everyone is working from the same starting point. By having clear boundaries applying rewards and consequences becomes significantly easier.

Rewards and consequences

Once we have changed the way the school refuser does things and we have established clear, firm and fair boundaries it is then time to talk about the rewards and consequences for maintaining or reneging on agreements made. As harsh as this may seem, the reality is that all of us live with boundaries and are rewarded or punished depending on whether we adhere to those boundaries. For example, when we have a job we have a start time, finish time and designated breaks. We are expected to complete certain tasks every day in a timely manner. These are our boundaries. If we choose to come in late every morning our employer may dock our pay, expect us to work through our lunch break or leave later at night. If we extend our lunch break without permission we may be given an official warning. Equally, if we come in early and work through our lunch break our employer may reward us with a bonus. This is the real world and learning to live within it is what distinguishes those who succeed from those who do not.

The first and most important thing to remember when determining rewards and consequences is that being at home when you should be at school should not be pleasant. If your child has access to a fridge full of goodies, all the electronics that money can buy, little if any responsibility to their school or family then why would they want to challenge themselves to return to school? At home there is no homework, social demands or academic expectations. Where is the motivation to get better? They are well within their comfort zone and quite happy to stay there.

When establishing rewards and consequences you must ensure that you are using a 'currency' that is valuable to your child and is age appropriate. It is, for example, of little value to withhold pocket money if the child has a bank account with their own money in it that they have amassed over several birthdays and other holidays. Similarly it is useless to offer

Internet time if they have unlimited access to it. Just like in the real world where we work to earn our 'currency' they too must learn that things like Internet time, iPad time or staying up late is earned.

Whenever I work with families to establish rewards and consequences, I ensure that we always work on rewards first. The child is always involved and encouraged to seek appropriate rewards for their efforts. By establishing rewards, first, we give the child something to aspire to. They may not be happy that they now need to earn their Internet time but it is better than having none. (Some examples of rewards and consequences that parents can use are provided in Chapter 5).

Exposure: Imaginal to in-vivo

Exposure therapy is a technique in behaviour therapy that is used to treat Anxiety Disorders. It is particularly effective for treating phobias as it exposes the person to the feared object or situation in a gradual and safe manner hence helping them to overcome their anxiety and distress. Depending on the severity of the anxiety, exposure can begin in-vivo (in the actual setting) or imaginal (where you imagine yourself in that setting). In-vivo exposure with school refusal might begin by getting the student to go to school for an hour every morning and sit in the library and then slowly venturing out to the playground and classes. If the anxiety were particularly severe, we would begin by having the student imagine themselves getting to school. The script for the guided exposure would look something like this (we start with a simple centring/mindfulness task to minimise anxiety):

- Close your eyes.
- Sit comfortably in your chair (or laying on your bed if at home).

- Take three long, slow deep breaths. Every time you breathe out tell yourself to relax.

- Listen to the sounds and sensations of your body (listen to your heart beat, become aware of the air going in and out of your nostrils).

- Feel your feet against the floor (or your back against the bed).

- Listen to the sounds in the room: the clock ticking, the walls creaking, the chair squeaking.

- Now listen to the sounds outside the room: traffic out on the road, birds chirping, wind blowing.

- Bring yourself back into the room and focus on those sounds again.

- Now focus on your breathing.

  I want you now to imagine yourself in bed and the alarm going off at 7 am as it always does on a school morning.

  You notice that as soon as you register that it's a school day you begin to feel anxious; your breathing grows more shallow, your mind begins to race, your stomach begins to feel sick. Once this would have set you off into a downward spiral but now you know that this is just your anxiety trying to take control:

- Take a few deep breaths and use your mantra to reaffirm the power you have within. Feel your mind and body calming itself. Feel the oxytocin release from your brain and flood your system rendering the cortisol inactive.

- In your calmed state get yourself out of bed. Have a big stretch and take another deep breath.

- Go to the bathroom, wash your face, look in the mirror and smile! Smile because you know you got this.

- Walk to the kitchen, greet everyone with a smile and a big 'good morning'. Eat breakfast. Keep a track of what your breathing is doing. Ensure that it stays deep, slow and rhythmical. If your mind begins (don't let it get out of control) to wander to the negative use your mantra, put on your favourite music and sing out loud.

- Go to the bathroom brush your teeth, comb your hair and go back to your room to get dressed. If you feel the anxiety creeping back in go back to your breathing, mantra, music or anything else that helps you refocus and maintain calm.

- Collect your bag, place your lunch in the bag and follow your mum/dad out to the car. As the anxiety begins to rise go back to your breathing, mantra, music. You are in control. You got this! As the car gets closer to school you may notice the anxiety trying to creep back in again but you got this, you know what to do. Take control and get it right.

- You realise you've made it all the way to school. Hooray for you! You're almost there. Yes the anxiety may be spiking but you got this. Get a hold of that anxiety, give it a good old fashioned noogy. You're the boss not the anxiety.

- You step out of the car, straighten your back, hold your head up high, take a big breath and take the first step towards the rest of your life. You got this tiger!

Guided exposures need to be tailored to the individual student's needs but you can see from this example that it exposes them to their fear of school in a safe and positive manner. The wonderful thing with guided exposure is that the more you engage in it the better you begin to feel. The brain learns through these repeated exposures that going to school does not need to generate fear or anxiety and that the student has the power, skills and resilience to achieve this goal. I often recommend that these guided exposures be conducted 3 to 4 times per day. It is amazing to watch the reduction in anxiety levels even after the first two or three exposures. As we would expect, there is a spike in symptomatology when we go from imaginal to in-vivo exposure but the impact is limited because the brain registers that it has done this before, with success, so why should this time be any different. Guided exposure is an excellent example of cognitive restructuring that we will discuss next.

Cognitive restructuring

Any good CBT program will incorporate cognitive restructuring. Cognitive restructuring is a therapeutic process that helps the person to identify and dispute irrational or maladaptive thoughts known as cognitive distortions. These distortions include all or nothing thinking, magical thinking, catastrophising and emotional reasoning.

All or nothing thinking is where the individual (in our case student) tends to think in extremes. Going to school is viewed as either all good or all bad with no middle ground. Their view on school is very much black and white. Because the student chooses to focus on all the bad things at school, they fail to see the good. If, for example, the school refusal started as a consequence of bullying, they cannot see past the bullying — school = bullying and nothing else.

'*Magical thinking*' is where the student believes that having a thought or engaging in an action will bring about some form of calamity. For example, many years ago I treated an 8-

year-old girl who had been taken to hospital by ambulance, while at school, for what was eventually diagnosed as a heart condition. Once recovered, this formerly friendly and studious young lady began refusing to go to school. Upon close investigation it was determined that she did not want to return to school because that's where she got sick and if she returned, school would make her sick again. While this line of reasoning may seem silly to the outsider, it is very real for the person concerned and must be worked with respectfully.

'*Catastrophising*' is also referred to as magnification or overreacting. This cognitive distortion causes the person to magnify the significance of an event or situation that produces a long-term negative response. In the case of the school refuser, one simple, singular event can become the focus and justification for school refusal. For example, a highly anxious 10-year-old boy began refusing school after his mother was caught in traffic resulting in him having to wait for her in the school office for approximately one hour. Although he was safe and knew what had held his mother up, he determined that it would happen again so refused to go to school.

'*Emotional reasoning*' refers to the person's belief that their emotional reaction to an event or situation proves that something is true regardless of the observed evidence. For example, the school refuser may have had an argument with their best friend and although the best friend has reassured the school refuser that 'all is good', the school refuser still feels hurt and uneasy so assumes that the friendship is over.

An important part of treating these cognitive distortions is to evoke 'cognitive dissonance', which was first termed by psychologist Leon Festinger. This term is used to describe the feelings of discomfort that result from holding two conflicting beliefs. In order to reduce dissonance, something must change. In the case of school refusal we posit alternative ways of processing their cognitive distortions in the hope that the student will then be forced to re-think their belief about a particular event or situation. For example, the school refuser who has fought with their best friend may be asked to provide evidence of the ongoing feud based on the friend's behaviour. We would hope that when the school refuser realises that they only have their emotional reasoning to base their beliefs in, it would produce enough dissonance to make them re-think the situation.

Some helpful tools for managing cognitive distortions include:

- Keep a diary of your cognitive distortions. Sometimes seeing, in writing, just how off target your thinking is can begin the process of change (see Figure 6.4 over the page for an example of what a thought diary could look like).

- Reality test the belief. Ask yourself 'how likely is this to happen?'

- Decatastrophise, also known as the 'What if ...' technique. Ask yourself, for example, 'What if I chose to actively work against my anxiety? What would happen then?'.

- List rational alternatives; for example, 'What are the rational reasons for my teacher getting angry at me?'.

'*Responsibility pie*' is a CBT tool for assessing how much control you have over a particular situation. Its purpose is to help the person understand that it is rarely just one thing that brought about the issue but rather a number of contributing factors. In the case of school refusal we can use a responsibility pie to help the student assess the relative importance of

Situation	Thought	Emotions	Behaviour	Alternative Thought
I haven't been to school for a month	• People are going to think I am weird and ask me why I was away.	• Embarrassed • Sad • Anxious	• Stay home. • Hide out in my room. • Pretend this really doesn't matter	• It is no one's business why I've been away. • If people ask what happened I'll just say I was unwell.
I have to go to school to get the results of the school assessed course-work (SAC) that I did last week	• I know I've failed it and I can't face the teacher lecturing me about being more focused	• Afraid • Anxious • Worried	• Unable to sleep at night. • Wake up feeling terrible. • Take the day off school.	• I did the best I could. • Even if I did fail maybe I can do a re-sit. • If I ask for help I know I'll get it.
Mum was late picking me up from school yesterday. She said she was stuck in traffic.	• She forgot me there. • She might forget me again. • I don't want to feel like that again.	• Fear • Angry • Worried • Anxious	• Wake up crying. • Swore at mum. • Felt sick. • Vomited just before we were due to go to school.	• Mum has never forgotten me and has never said she doesn't love me. • What happened last night was unavoidable. • I was safe and warm in the front office.

Figure 6.4 Example thought diary

each of the factors. The following step-by-step guide progresses a student through a responsibility pie:

- Step 1: Have the student tell you what their main reason for not attending school is; for example, a fight with friends.

- Step 2: Have the student rate this out of 100% (or if student is very young then out of 10); at this step, the student will be likely to attribute a very high percentage to this reason.

- Step 3: Get them to think of several other reasons (as many as they can think of) that they may have for not going to school and have them list these additional reasons under the main reason.

- Step 4: Give them a piece of paper with a circle on it.

- Step 5: Ask them to start at the BOTTOM of their list and have them apportion the circle into slices of pie showing what percentage each of these reasons are attributable to them not attending school.

- Step 6: Ask the student to look at the pie and have them notice what percentage is now attributable to the main reason that they stated at the beginning of the task.

We would expect that the percentage attributed to their main reason is significantly less than when the student initially started the task. In the example provided in Figure 6.5, fighting with friends was noted as the main reason for not attending school when we started the exercise, but after attributing percentages and apportioning pieces of pie for the other reasons, the main reason has diminished to 15% by the end!

Responsibility pies are an effective way of challenging all cognitive distortions by introducing cognitive dissonance.

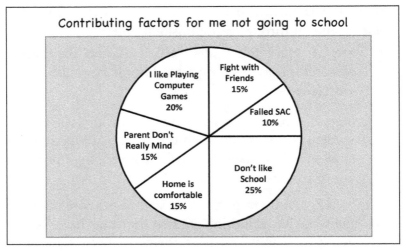

Figure 6.5 Example responsibility pie

Medication

There is no coincidence that medication has been relegated to the bottom of the treatment options to be considered when dealing with a school refuser. While medication has an important role to play in returning anxious students to school, it should only be considered when all other treatment options have been exhausted.

Medication is prescribed by the family GP, paediatrician or child psychiatrist and is used to ease anxiety symptoms sufficiently to make a return to school possible. Medication should be used as an adjunct to other treatment options, rather than a stand-alone treatment, as it rarely produces long-term gains because the student has not learnt to manage their anxiety but rather how to mask it. Medication is generally prescribed for 6 to 12 months during which time it is assumed that the student will actively engage in self-management practices to ensure that medication is not required long term.

It is important to remember that medication comes with its own set of problems and is not a panacea for school refusal. Often desperate and frustrated parents look for a quick fix and can be led to believe (by media and some health professionals) that this is possible with medication. While medication will certainly help reduce levels of anxiety it does nothing towards overcoming the phobia associated with returning to school. Like any task that is avoided for long periods of time we have to expect discomfort when we re engage. For example, if we, as adults, have a long break from work (e.g., long service leave) we all know that the first few days back are difficult and tiring. No amount of medication stops this happening.

Medication also needs time to take effect, so if you're hoping to take some type of medication today and be better tomorrow, think again. Antidepressant and anxiolytic medications can take up to six weeks to reach therapeutic levels. These medications also come with side effects that need to be taken into consideration and may include headaches, nausea, drowsiness, dizziness, sleep disturbance, irritability, dry mouth, and in rare cases, suicidality. Side effects are not the same for everyone and most people experience few, if any, but it is still important to be aware of possible ill effects when taking these medications.

Alternatives to prescribed medications

As our society has become more educated about prescribed medications and their possible adverse side effects, I have found that families often seek alternative treatments to assist with their own and their child's management of anxiety. Over the years I have noticed that two alternatives to prescribed medications are regularly used by clients: a solution of distilled flower essences (the most popular is 'Rescue Remedy™', which is a commercially branded product and available over the counter), and the mineral magnesium taken as a supplement.

Rescue Remedy™ claims to be beneficial in assisting with anxiety and sleep. If this product is being considered as an alternative to other forms of medication(s) or included with existing medications, you must discuss this with your GP before use to ensure that there are no known adverse interactions with any other medications or supplements your child is taking.

Magnesium is a naturally occurring mineral in the body that, among other things, regulates the nervous system and aids in stress management. If your child suffers from a magnesium deficiency as shown from a simple blood test, you might find a recommended dosage used as a supplement to be beneficial. Again, it is important that you consult your GP first.

Chapter 7

Treating high achievers who are school refusing

Whenever I have been asked to speak about school refusal I am inevitably asked about high achievers who for no apparent reason begin refusing school. I therefore felt it would be wise to discuss in some detail why this happens, strategies that work best for this group and how we, as parents, teachers and health professionals, can best support them.

What are high achievers you ask? This is that small group of older students who always perform in the top 1% or 2% of the class and are diligent and focused. They are often the 'school prefects' who get award after award for academic excellence and effort. They are respected by teachers and students alike and are often, although not always, heavily involved in extracurricular activities. Although there are no diagnostic criteria in the DSM-5 that specifically recognises this group, we all know at least one student who starts off as the trailblazer and then suddenly begins to develop symptoms that keep them away from school for longer and longer periods of time.

The symptoms of the high achieving school refuser are no different to other school refusers. The difference, however, lies in what drives the school refusal. The students in this group have an insatiable need to perform at their best with few, if any, errors. These are the students who become distressed because their results in ONE exam have dropped to below a high distinction. They are without a doubt their own worst enemy.

This group have an enormous fear of failure and do not respond well to anything except praise and perfect scores. Their need to be recognised for their contributions are foremost in their minds. I once met a young woman who in addition to Year 12 was also involved in the school band, school musical and the debating team! All this plus expecting herself to achieve an Australian Tertiary Admission Rank (ATAR) in the 90s! It is perhaps of no surprise that when I met her she was having trouble sleeping, mood swings, stomach upsets, migraines and more. As service providers and parents, it is important that we identify these students quickly and intervene with appropriate treatment options otherwise burn out and failure are highly likely.

In addition to doing too much, this group also tend to present with a lack of balance in their life. I find that this group often have little left in their life other than study. While it is important that study be made a priority in the final years of high school it cannot and must not be the ONLY thing. All of us need balance in our lives and students are no different. They need to be encouraged to seek out social interaction and engage in exercise or sport to keep their mind and body healthy. I often recommend that one day and one night per week be made homework free and to use that time to hang out with friends and do fun and re energising activities like going to the movies, going out for coffee, hanging out at a friend's house, watch movies, play soccer/football/basketball. In short, anything that takes them away from the pressures of being a student and allows them to just be kids.

Often parents do not understand that long hours of study do not make them productive hours of study. The human brain is not geared to remain focussed for hours and hours at a time. There is no coincidence that classes at school and university run for 50 to 60 minutes and when they run for longer short breaks to 'stretch your legs' are encouraged. These students are already highly strung about their performance and grades and do not need the added pressure of needing to show that they are studying extra hard to achieve perfect grades. In fact, I have found that long hours of study increase fear and anxiety leading to ineffectual use of time (because they stop absorbing information) and an increase in frustration and negative self-talk (because they feel they are not achieving). This is a vicious cycle that can be easily avoided if the student is encouraged to take short breaks during their study time and have longer breaks where they can just be kids.

By virtue of their need to be academically outstanding this group tends to engage in lots of cognitive distortion. In their mind anything below a high distinction is as good as a fail and they genuinely believe that people will not respect them if they are doing anything less than they have in the past. In recent years I have worked with several senior school students who are typical of this group. The following case example highlights some of the issues that a student in this group will experience.

Case example

Rachel was in Year 12 at a local private school. She is an only child with professional parents who are divorced and re-partnered. She was brought in with symptoms of severe anxiety and a long history of intermittent school refusal since Year 10. At our first meeting Rachel told me with pride that she had always achieved high grades in primary school and that studying had come naturally for her. Even when she began high school she reported that while her friends struggled with new concepts she continued to achieve high grades. She reported getting awards for academic excellence in Years 7, 8 and 9 and was shattered when in Year 10 she did not receive one. In our discussions over the ensuing weeks, it became apparent that Rachel had always found school easy until she reached her senior years. She had developed a reputation within her school for being 'a brainiac' and began to find it hard to accept that, for the first time in her short life, she was struggling to grasp concepts and consequently not doing as well as she had in the past. Her situation was made worse by her well meaning parents who expected her to keep up her grades and 'make them proud', and her school who 'knew that she could pick up her game' if she would only keep trying.

In short, the combination of Rachel's perfectionistic tendencies, her parents' expectations and her school's misguided attempt at support, brought about the slow but gradual onset of anxiety and school refusal. Rachel's mother reported that she too had noted that the older Rachel had become the less she was going to school. This, of course, is logical because the older Rachel became the greater the expectations and effort required to maintain her grades. When I met Rachel she was achieving average grades and at approximately 40% attendance. Rachel had become a master of manipulation to avoid school and would get up and prepare to go to school only to call her mother just as she'd arrived at work to tell her that she was unable to attend to school. As her mother was not in a position to come home and get her to school, Rachel would achieve another day off school. Rachel's mother admitted that she had given up on getting Rachel to school and that Rachel was not even attempting to get up in the mornings.

Upon reflection, Rachel agreed that she was struggling with her less-than-perfect grades and had not allowed for the possibility that a day would come where she would actually have to work hard to achieve excellence. She admitted that she was even questioning whether she wanted to go to university because she 'couldn't be bothered with the work'. She claimed to want to return to school but several attempts to return fell far short of the goals agreed on and eventually it was decided that she would seek employment for the remainder of the year and undertake TAFE courses the following year. I often wonder how the trajectory of this young girl's life could have been changed if intervention had been sought earlier.

Treatment strategies for high achievers

In addition to the strategies discussed in Chapter 6, the additional approaches discussed in this chapter can be helpful for this high achievers group.

Effective use of a diary

The effective use of diaries can be a highly efficient and stress reducing process. Most students I meet have been taught to write their homework into their diaries but little beyond that. I recommend that each day be ruled into the following four column sections that are filled in at the end of each class:

- Column 1 = Subject
- Column 2 = Details of homework set
- Column 3 = Due date
- Column 4 = Estimated time to complete homework plus 30 minutes.

This system allows the student to see at a glance exactly what needs to be done and when. I have found that high achievers often lack the ability to prioritise and feel the need to complete their homework when it is assigned. This creates anxiety that is not necessary and rarely results in quality work. By having a due date and estimated time to complete the work, they can be taught the importance of prioritisation and to ration large projects and tackle smaller tasks as they near their due date.

Year planners

Year planners are a natural flow on from effective use of diaries. I always recommend large poster-sized planners that are kept wherever the student does their work. Year planners are a great way of keeping due dates in mind and planning accordingly. Unlike diaries that are either a day to a page or a week to an opening, year planners give a complete view of the entire year at a glance. There are no nasty surprises with year planners. No gut wrenching anxiety when you turn the page on your weekly diary and find that you have an assignment due the following week. I recommend additions to the year planner on a daily basis. This only takes a minute or two each day but provides enormous control and stability. The main benefits of a year planner are illustrated in Figure 7.1

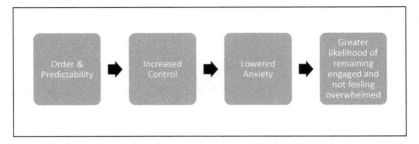

Figure 7.1 Benefits of a year planner

Study plans

Study plans are an organised schedule that students create to keep their ongoing commitments, study times and learning goals in balance. Study plans are essential for this group as they often have unrealistic expectations of what can be achieved in one day. This is the reason why emphasis is placed on the fourth column of their diary (estimated time to complete plus 30 minutes). The additional 30 minutes allows for short breaks and ineffectual use of time, which I explain, happens to everyone.

The first step in establishing a workable study plan is to determine current commitments and block those out. This would include rosters for work, extra curricula activities and outings with friends. We then block out study periods and allocate specific learning goals to that time (i.e., complete first draft of English SAC – 90 minutes). It is important that we allow time for eating dinner with family, having showers and taking short breaks, into the study periods, as it is easy for these students to become so engrossed in their study that they become isolated and withdrawn. I find that this system not only assists with homework organisation and time management but it also quickly highlights when a student is working too many hours in their part time job, engaging in too many extra curricula activities to 'not let people down' or expectations exceed hours in a day.

Study plans can be completed weekly or fortnightly depending on work rosters or sports training schedules and are used in conjunction with school diaries and year planners. An example of a weekly study plan is shown in Figure 7.2 over the page.

The study plan displayed is a typical example and can be modified to reflect the student's day. The time taken to complete a weekly or fortnightly study plan is more than justified when we consider the benefits to the student. I often recommend that study plans be shared with parents so that they too are aware of the student's commitments and do not add to the student's already extensive commitments. Parents are also able to use study plans and year diaries to ensure that their child is engaging in a healthy mix of study and play.

Although I have already alluded to the importance of family and school expectations in this chapter, I think it bears saying again. We as health professionals owe it to these students to ascertain what the expectations of parents and teachers are. If the student is under pressure to be exceptional and experiences disapproval when their grades are less than perfect this will, without doubt, add to the student's stress and anxiety. I have worked with many students who are constantly reminded of the sacrifices parents are making to put them through school, and the academic expectations of students by school staff and governing bodies (especially private schools) who believe that the student will bolster a school's ratings therefore ranking them as a more desirable school. There is a fine line between believing in the student and putting undue pressure on the student. There are many pathways to achieving our academic goals, let's keep that in mind when we deal with these high achievers.

	Monday	Tuesday	Wednesday	Thursday	Friday	Saturday	Sunday
9.00–10.00	School	School	School	School	Homework	Work	Free Time
10.00–11.00	School	School	School	School	School	Work	Homework
11.00–12.00	School	School	School	School	School	Work	Homework
12.00–1.00	School	Lunch	School	School	School	Work	Homework
1.00–2.00	School	Homework	School	School	School	Work	Homework
2.00–3.00	School	Homework	School	School	School	Work	Homework
3.00–4.00	School	Homework	School	School	School	Work	Homework
4.00–5.00	Free Time	Homework	Free Time	Free Time	Homework	Work	Free Time
5.00–6.00	Homework	Free Time	Homework	Work	Homework	Work	Free Time
6.00–7.00	Homework	Free Time	Homework	Work	Homework	Free Time	Free Time
7.00–8.00	Dinner	Dinner	Dinner	Work	Dinner	Free Time	Dinner
8.00–9.00	Homework	Free Night	Homework	Free Time	Free Time	Free Time	Homework
9.00–10.00	Homework	Free Night	Homework	Free Time	Free Time	Free Time	Homework
10.00–11.00	Bed Time	Bed Time	Bed Time	Bed Time	Bed Time	Free Time	Bed Time

Figure 7.2 Example weekly study plan

As a parting word of advice I would advise that because these students are quite high functioning it is essential that they understand what is happening to them and why. I spend more time on **psychoeducation** and **cognitive distortions** with this group as they need to 'get it' before they engage in treatment.

Chapter 8

Treating students with Autism Spectrum Disorder (ASD) who are school refusing

Anxiety disorder and ASD tend to go hand in hand. Most ASD students will, at some point in their academic life, experience complex and severe anxiety that can, and often does, impact on school attendance. In addition to the reasons already discussed for school refusal this group also deal with sensory overload. Most students have no problems organising sensory information they get from their environment but students with sensory processing deficits struggle with it. Sensory overload in students with ASD occurs when the normal day-to-day stimuli in the environment becomes overpowering and produce feelings of frustration and overwhelm. Lights, smells, sounds and texture are just a few of the things that can set off an ASD student. Sadly, the impact of sensory overload is often poorly understood by parents and teachers, which can aggravate an already precarious situation. When describing sensory overload I always use the following example:

> Imagine that from the minute you wake up in the morning all the sensory input from your environment harms you. The light coming on in your bedroom does not just wake you but jolts you into reality. The temperature difference between being in bed and getting out of bed is a further shock (like shards of ice piercing your skin). The school jumper and pants are rough and scratchy and no matter how hard you try your concentration is drawn back to the itch. The comb through your hair makes you cringe. The toothbrush and toothpaste in your mouth feel invasive and burning. Then you arrive in the kitchen to find that your toast is cut the wrong way and your sibling is sitting in your seat. You feel the anger rise, the frustration

build and the injustice of it all is too much. BANG! Meltdown number one for the day begins! If you are lucky your mum knows how to soothe your meltdowns and you manage to get in the car in a semi-relaxed state but then as the car starts to move it all begins again: the feeling of the car moving, the noise and movement of traffic, the conversations in the car, the radio in the background. Your anxiety begins to elevate and you begin to feel overwhelmed, before you can get a handle on this environment mum stops the car and tells you that she'll see you tonight. Your pulse races as you step out of the car and into the insanity that is your schoolyard. Children running, friends calling out to you, the bright light of day, and the smells that can only come from so many people being in close proximity to one another. You begin to feel hot as you make your way to the class-room. The bell rings and reverberates through every fibre of your being. You scream inside your head — 'let me out of here'. You finally make it to class and meltdown number two for the day is triggered when the teacher tells you not to push into the front of the line and all you can think is — 'but the front of the line means I don't have to look at the whole class fidgeting and talking. 'Why doesn't anyone understand!'. You begin to scream and curse and suddenly you see all eyes on you and your teacher is telling you she's 'not doing this again'. That she's not going to allow you to ruin yet another day and to get yourself to the principal's office.

As you walk away you can feel all those eyes burning into your soul and you feel ashamed, scared and sad. You reach the principal's office and sit out the front, as you always do, and await the lecture that will surely come but the upside is that you don't feel so overwhelmed here. There aren't as many things to make you feel overwhelmed and slowly but surely you begin to feel a semblance of normal return. You look up at the clock and its 9.10 am! You have six-and-a-half hours of this left!

In addition to the sensory overload, this group also deals with friendship issues, academic deficits such as comprehension and expression and emotional dysregulation. To say school is a challenge for this group is a gross underestimation, and keeping them at school takes a concerted effort by teachers, parents and other health professionals.

Strategies for managing school refusal in autism spectrum disorder students

In addition to the various strategies previously discussed, the following strategies may enhance the probability of re-engagement as they focus on reducing stress and sensory overload.

Photo sequencing

ASD students respond well to highly structured routines as they facilitate a sense of control and stability. Setting up a structured morning routine can assist in an easier transition from home to school. I prefer to use photo sequencing as this encourages independence while also minimising interaction that could set off a meltdown. Photo sequencing is simply a series of photos of the student at each step of their morning routine. The photos can either be placed in the relevant rooms (i.e., bedroom, bathroom, kitchen) or placed in a small photo album in sequential order. Photo sequencing needs to be mindful of the student's sensitivities to avoid overwhelm and meltdown. A typical photo sequence would be as follows:

- Photo 1: Alarm set to 7 am (or whatever time the student gets up).

- Photo 2: Parent/caregiver turning on bedside lamp (if overhead lights are deemed a trigger for meltdown).

- Photo 3: Student getting up and going to toilet.

- Photo 4: Student returning to their bedroom and dressing.

- Photo 5: Student making their bed (if required).

- Photo 6: Student coming to the kitchen and sitting down to breakfast or making their own breakfast (keep this consistent).

- Photo 7: Student loading dishes into the dishwasher or washing their own dishes and placing in the dish rack (keep this consistent).

- Photo 8: Student putting lunch and schoolbooks into school bag.

- Photo 9: Student brushing teeth (with whatever tooth-paste they find palatable).

- Photo 10: Student brushing hair (with whatever brush is deemed appropriate).

- Photo 11: Student engaging in a reward activity if they have completed 1 to 10 in the sequence before going to school time.

- Photo 12: Student walking to car with bag in hand.

The wonderful part of this technique is that the student is encouraged to work towards their reward (photo 11) with little, if any, involvement by parents. I have seen this technique work well with both children and teenagers and can turn a morning of yelling and screaming into a pleasant and stress free event. The key to success is obviously the reward in Photo 11. This reward is only gained AFTER their routine is completed and is only available until it is time to go to school. Failure to disengage on time results in agreed upon consequences for that evening (for example, less time on I-Pad) or the following morning (for example, earlier wake up time).

The following case example illustrates photo sequencing in action.

Case example

Raymond is an 11-year-old boy diagnosed with ASD and living with his single mother (Lidia) who works full time. Upon referral, Lidia explains that every morning is stressful, as Raymond hates getting ready for school so dawdles through his routine. She confesses to dressing Raymond when she becomes desperate. When I ask Raymond what his 'favourite thing in the world is', he tells me that he loves playing down ball which he plays at recess and lunchtime with his one and only friend or alone. When I ask if he plays down ball at home he informs me that there is no time for down ball at home because he and Lidia arrive home just in time for dinner. I ask Raymond if he'd like to play more down ball and therefore become an even better player, and he jumps at the opportunity. I explain that he can play down ball every morning before school as long as he finishes his morning routine and is ready to leave by 8.30 am. At their second appointment two weeks later Lidia and Raymond inform me that while there were some teething problems in the first few days, Raymond had successfully established his routine and was playing an average of 45 minutes of down ball each morning! This was an enormous change from the screaming and tears (from both Lidia and Raymond) that were reported at their first session and Raymond admitted that it was nice to get to the car without having been yelled at. We later established an evening photo sequence that was also quite successful.

Arriving to school early

Easing the ASD student into their school day by arriving early can be time effective and less traumatic. Arriving even 20 minutes early often means less traffic in the drop off area, fewer students in the school grounds and less stress about arriving to their classroom or locker by the designated time. Where possible have the student enter their classroom early to assist their teacher with setting up for the day or to feed the classroom pet or tend to the classroom veggie garden. Activities such as this give the student a sense of purpose and a feeling of control. By the time other students arrive the ASD student is calmer and less stressed than having to hurry from home to car, from car to class.

Daily timetables

Providing the ASD student with a daily timetable that highlights any changes that will occur during the day can significantly reduce the likelihood of outbursts and meltdowns. We need to remember that ASD students do not cope well with change and what may appear insignificant to us is just one more sensory/emotional issue that the student must cope with. Something as simple as an art class in a different room, or an emergency teacher taking PE may cause feelings of overwhelm and confusion. The more information the student has about their day the more 'in control' they feel. If the student is arriving early this could be one of the activities they engage in to ease into their day.

Social stories

Social stories are a concept devised by Carol Gray in 1991 to improve the social skills of people with ASD. Social stories model appropriate social interaction by describing a situation with relevant social cues, other people's perspectives and suggested appropriate social responses. Using social stories to introduce new social situations that may be encountered in the ASD student's day will not only improve their social skills but will also provide a framework for the student to work within hence reducing stress, anxiety and potential meltdowns. If for example, there is a requirement to work in a group setting, using a social story to talk about the setting that the group work will occur in, who and where people will sit, what the topic of conversation will be, what to expect from other people and how to respond appropriately (i.e. turn taking; keeping eye contact, inside voice) will significantly reduce distress in that situation.

Social stories are best used shortly before the interaction rather than days or weeks before, as the student is likely to forget. It is always a good idea to have the student repeat the social story to ensure understanding and reinforce learning. Social stories can be verbal, pictorial (drawings, photos) or imaginal (imagine yourself in this situation).

An example of a social story:

> Today you will be working in small groups on your history assignment. Your class will be held in the library and you will be working with your friends Billy and John. Although the small groups will be scattered throughout the library it may get noisy so it may be a good idea to use your earplugs to block out some of the noise. When we work in groups we respect everybody's opinion and everyone gets a say. Everyone can

take a turn at writing down ideas or you can elect someone to do all the note taking.

When Billy or John is speaking, it is important that you sit quietly and listen attentively. It is ok to ask questions once they have finished talking. You will be given a turn to have your say and then Billy and John will have an opportunity to ask you questions. If you begin to feel anxious, angry or confused you can show your teacher your red card and leave the library to get a drink, go to the toilet or just sit quietly outside until you feel better. You can try doing your breathing exercises, playing with your fidget toy, or getting a drink of water. Don't forget though that you'll need to come back to the library within 15 minutes.

Sensory rooms or areas

Sensory rooms are small areas within a classroom or in a school that a specifically allocated and furnished to accommodate the sensory needs of children with special needs. In junior school a sensory area can be a corner of the classroom cordoned off by two bookshelves, an indoor tent or plastic fortress. In middle and senior school the sensory area can be a small room near the school counsellor's office or year level coordinator. What is placed in these rooms is as varied as the children who use them. I often suggest the inclusion of items such as:

- weighted blankets and vests
- fidget toys such as spinners, rubber/stretchy toys, textured balls, textured fabrics, stuffed toys
- mandala colouring books
- puzzles
- a variety of music.

Small storage boxes with the student's name clearly displayed could be used to hold items that are specifically useful to THAT student. For example, earplugs, sunglasses, affirmation cards, family photos, special books, and so on.

It is best to avoid electronics in sensory rooms as ASD students can become quickly engrossed and may find it difficult to disengage. If the room is carefully supervised electronics could be considered but only if strict guidelines are in place.

Identify triggers and warnings

Helping the student to learn what sets them off and how to identify the early warning signs that their body gives to alert them to impending meltdowns is an essential part of learning self-regulatory behaviour. I request the student, parents/caregivers and significant teachers (i.e., those who work with the student most) to complete a triggers and warnings sheet. The sheet asks two simple questions:

1. What physical signs do you see that precede a meltdown?
2. What places and situations set this student off?

I always request that each person complete this task in isolation in order to get as full a picture as possible. Once the task is completed I then request that the warnings be categorised based on sequence of appearance. The target is to identify the FIRST sign of impending meltdown. This is best done by working backwards from the obvious signs of meltdown, to those often subtle early signs that the student is not coping. The information gathered from this task is then disseminated to everyone working with the student to ensure that everyone is looking for the early warning signs and not allowing situations to get out of control.

I then complete the exercise with the student. For example, the student may identify five things they feel in their body when they are about to have a meltdown. We put these five signs in order from 'what's happening in my body *just before* I have a meltdown' to 'what I feel when I start to get distressed'.

The student is then taught to seek help at 'starting to get distressed'. This could include showing a red card to leave the room and practise their mindfulness or breathing exercises or going to the welfare coordinator to have them assist. Either way the student feels more in control and empowered and less likely to allow the symptoms to escalate.

The identification of situations and places (triggers) that set the student off is also essential as this allows the student, parents and teachers to prepare in advance. If, for example, everyone agrees that the noise in the assembly hall is a trigger, the student can be given earplugs on the way to assembly to minimise the impact of the noise hence diminishing the possibility of meltdown.

Small group play

Social interaction and establishing friendships are amongst the biggest challenges faced by the ASD student and can be one of the biggest reasons that they refuse to attend school. Unless a teacher is particularly attuned to his/her students needs the temptation is to encourage the ASD student to play outside with all the other children. If, however, we remember how easily overwhelmed these students become it becomes logical to encourage small group play instead. This may take a little planning on the part of the teacher but the reward is a calm and happy student after recess and lunchtime. Some suggestions for small group play could include establishing:

- chess club
- gardening group
- clean-up crew
- down ball team
- book club

- exercise class

- mindfulness class

The list of possibilities is endless and is not just beneficial for the ASD student.

Visual learning

ASD students often have comorbid auditory processing deficits that impact on the way they learn. This means that anything that is presented/described in an auditory manner is likely to get scrambled when it is processed. The answer, wherever possible, is to provide visual learning.

If, for example, the class is learning multiplication it might be best to teach the ASD student this concept using visual cues. For example, three multiplied by five (3×5) is presented as three circles on the table with five **tactile** items in each circle that are then counted to give the answer — 15. While this may not produce the volume of work that other students complete it is more likely to be learnt and remembered by the ASD student.

Managing school assignments and homework

Many ASD students are highly intelligent but have difficulty getting their ideas on paper. For this reason, it is best that schoolwork is parcelled in small, workable amounts, which the student can present in whatever format suits their learning. Being able to complete work (even if it is 50% of what their cohort are completing) builds self-confidence and encourages long-term learning. Being able to present their work in a manner that facilitates expression is also important. I have found that some older ASD students find it easier to complete assignment work with the assistance of word recognition software such as Dragon Speak, which allows for expression of ideas without the need to write them down.

Many parents of ASD students express concern and exasperation at their child's unwillingness to complete regular homework. If we consider this from the student's perspective it is understandable as they struggle all day to keep it together while at school and the thought of more of the same when they get home horrifies them. Some schools, however, have a regular homework policy that the student needs to develop and adhere to. I find the best way to introduce homework is to start small with clear rewards for completion. Begin with 10 minutes per night either before or after dinner with a parent/carer present and directing tasks for that time. It is important that once homework time is set it is adhered to *every* night without fail in order to establish it as part of the evening routine. We need to remember that ASD students cope best when the environment and expectations are consistent and clear. This may be inconvenient for parents but essential if we expect the ASD student to develop good study habits. Sadly I meet many families who wait until senior school before study habits are addressed and often, by then, behaviour is so ingrained that change is extremely difficult. Study habits are best started early so that Years 10 to 12 are just a continuation of already well established patterns. Increases in homework time need to be in small increments that are easily achieved and praised by both parents and teachers. An increase of 10 minutes may not seem like much to a parent or teacher but a huge achievement to an ASD student who has done little, if any, homework before. The rewards used to encourage homework completion need to be tailored to the individual student and delivered as close as possible to completion of homework or within the same evening.

The low arousal approach

The low arousal approach[1] emphasises the use of behaviour management strategies (discussed earlier in Chapter 6 and in this chapter) that focus on the reduction of stress, fear and frustration in order to prevent aggression and crisis situations. The basic premise of the low arousal approach is that any consequences for inappropriate behaviour are best delivered when the ASD student has calmed down and is no longer a threat to themselves or anyone else. This is in stark contrast to dealing with other students where we are encouraged to keep the consequence as close as possible to the behaviour so that the student is not confused about why they are receiving a consequence.

If we consider that the ASD student is already highly agitated, overstimulated and unable to process verbal stimuli accurately, we begin to understand why consequences need to be delayed until a reasonable degree of calm has been regained. This does not mean that the student 'gets away' with what they have done or that we abandon the need for consistency of approach and boundary setting, it just means that we allow the student to settle BEFORE we calmly and briefly discuss the consequences that have previously been agreed to. The following example may help to illustrate:

> Raymond is trying to work on his maths worksheet but is finding it hard to concentrate because the classroom is busy with activity and the sun is shining brightly on his desk. He has tried to get the teacher's attention to ask if the blind can be drawn but she is busy and has told him to 'hold on' on two separate occasions. Raymond begins to fidget in his seat (a clear warning sign) and starts scribbling on his worksheet out of frustration. As the teacher walks towards him and notices the scribbling she loudly (embarrassing for Raymond) and forcefully (frightening and threatening for Raymond) reprimands him for destroying his work. She then reminds him that they agreed last week that if he destroyed any of his work he would be banned from playing LEGO® in his free time for the remainder of the week. Raymond becomes visibly agitated and as he tries to pull his red card out to request 'time out' the teacher admonishes him for trying to get out of his consequence by 'playing his red card'. Raymond stands to

leave his chair and in the process tips his chair over scaring himself and the children near him. He storms out of the room cursing, screaming and crying. The teacher is obliged to follow, which makes him break into a run.

As we can see in this example, Raymond's teacher had several opportunities to minimise or completely stop the outburst that occurs. She could have:

- noticed the sun on his desk and moved him to a less sunny part of the room
- drawn the blind and left him where he was sitting
- encouraged him to wear his earplugs in order to minimise auditory overload
- encouraged him to work in a quiet corner facing away from the class in order to minimise visual overload
- noticed him fidgeting in his chair.

The final straw for Raymond is the withdrawal of his free LEGO® time in the midst of all the sensory issues he was trying to manage leading up to the outburst. If, however, his teacher had noticed the damaged worksheet and calmly encouraged Raymond to withdraw to his sensory area and discussed consequences when Raymond was calm, we may have had a different outcome.

In a home setting Raymond may knock over his mother's favourite vase while playing with a ball, which he knows, is not allowed and results in no electronics for that day. Most mothers in this situation would become angry and demand that Raymond bring all his electronics to the kitchen counter as he will not be using them until tomorrow. While the anger is understandable, it is guaranteed to inflame the situation and result in a significant meltdown that may take hours to resolve. If instead Raymond's mother sends him to his room, gives him time to calm down and then reminds him of his consequence, he is less likely to have a meltdown. He may become angry and yell and sulk but a full-blown meltdown is unlikely, as the sensory overload experienced when he smashes the vase has passed.

Down time

ASD students work very hard to keep it together while at school and breathe a sigh of relief when their school day ends. It is therefore advisable to provide the student down time immediately after school. It is not advisable to plan extracurricular activities immediately after school whether they are for the ASD student or siblings. It may appear acceptable to have your ASD child wait in the car to 'chill' while his sister attends a 45-minute dance class but in reality we are asking that ASD child to hold it together beyond their limits. Many parents report meltdowns at these times, which are understandable when you consider the stress that the extra 45 minutes places on the ASD child. By way of analogy, imagine that you have been holding on to go to the toilet all afternoon because your day has been frantic. You are driving home and just a few minutes away. Your phone rings and your partner asks that you pick up bread and milk from the supermarket. How would you feel? Now double those feelings many times over and you begin to understand how important it is for the ASD child to get relief from the pressures of their day. While I would never discourage extracurricular activities that the student enjoys I would suggest that they be arranged AFTER down time at home.

Phone and tablet apps to assist with expression of emotions and promote relaxation

Most ASD students have difficulty expressing and understanding emotions, which causes problems when trying to make friends, and in other social settings. Given that most ASD students have an inherent fascination with technology, it is in our best interests, as parents, teachers and service providers, to use this fascination to better equip the ASD student to manage emotions and situations that they often struggle with. A quick search of the Internet produces hundreds of apps that assist with the expression of emotions, enhance relaxation, and provide social stories to ease the student into upcoming social settings. I have provided a short list of free ASD apps that I have found useful at the end of this book but encourage you to seek apps that may be better suited to your child or student.

The use of emotions cards can also be beneficial in assisting ASD students to express how they are feeling and consequently diminish distress. The 'Stones Have Feelings Too' cards, by St Luke's Innovative Resources, are a powerful tool that encourages ASD students to find words that fit their feelings. I am often astounded at how many feelings are expressed with and without emotions cards. Many times I have asked the question, 'How are you feeling today?', and get 'ok' as a response, but then when asked to select how they are feeling based on feeling cards get 10 to 20 emotions that would never have come up in conversation.

Emotions sheets are also available on the Internet and can be downloaded free of charge. These sheets make excellent placemats that families can use to stimulate conversation and discuss how each member has felt during their day. Emotions sheets can also be cut down to individual emotions and laminated to produce booklets that younger ASD students can use to communicate how they are feeling to teachers and parents.

ASD when coupled with school refusal is complex and difficult to resolve. Sadly many ASD students disengage at some point in their education because their condition is misunderstood and poorly managed. For this reason it is essential that intervention be started as soon as disengagement begins, and a multidisciplinary team approach be encouraged.

Books & Websites

Aisbett. B. (Ed.). (2013). *Living with "IT": A survivor's guide to panic disorder.* Australia: Harper Collins.

Anxiety Disorders Association of Victoria (ADAVIC) Website. https://www.adavic.org.au/

Culbert, T., & Kajander, R. (2007). *Being the boss of your stress: Self-care for kids.* Minneapolis, MN: Free Spirit Publishing Inc.

Deal, R & Masman, K (2003). *Stones have feelings too.* Bendigo, Victoria: St Luke's Innovative Resources.

Eikov Green, S. (2010). *Don't pick on me: Help for kids to stand up to and deal with bullies.* Oakland, CA: Instant Help Books.

Field, E. M. (1999). B*ully busting: How to help children deal with teasing and bullying.* Sydney, Australia: Finch Publishing.

Huebner, D. (2006). *What to do when you worry too much: A kid's guide to overcoming anxiety.* Washington, DC: Magination Press.

Ironside, V. (1996). *The huge bag of worries.* London, England: Hodder Children's Books.

Johnston, N. (2008). *Go away, Mr worrythoughts!* Victoria, Australia: Nicky's Art Publishing.

Johnston, N. (2009). *Happythoughts are everywhere.* Victoria, Australia: Nicky's Art Publishing.

Kids Health Website. https://kidshealth.org/

O'Neill, C. (1993). *Relax.* Croatia: Child's Play.

Apps

Smiling Mind (Apple and Google Play Store)

Stress Check – Aiir Consulting LLC (Apple Store)

Sleep stream lite (Apple Store)

Moody Me – Mood diary and tracker (Apple Store)

Walk up alarm clock – smart ant Ricky Ho (Apple Store)

Resources specifically for ASD
Books

Baker, J. (2001). *The social skills picture book. Teaching play, emotion, and communication to children with autism.* Arlington, TX. Future Horizons Inc.

Diamond, S. & Gordon, A (2011). *Social Rules for Kids. The top 100 social rules kids need to succeed.* Shawnee Mission, Kansas: AAPC Publishing

Gray, C. (2010). *The new social story book.* Arlington, TX: Future Horizons

Hartman, D. (2015). *The growing up guide for girls. What girls on the autism spectrum need to know.* London, UK: Jessica Kingsley Publishers.

Hartman, D. (2015). The growing up book for boys. *What boys on the autism spectrum need to know.* London, UK: Jessica Kingsley Publishers.

Musgrave, F. (2017). *The Asperger teen's toolkit.* Philadelphia, PA: Jessica Kingsley Publishers.

Terban, M. (1983). *In a pickle and other funny idioms.* New York: Clarion Books.

Apps

Autism Xpress (Apple Store)

Kindergarten.com – Emotions (Apple Store)

Chapter 1

1. American Psychiatric Association. (2013). *Diagnostic and statistical manual of mental disorders* (5th ed.). Arlington, VA: Author.

2. Anxiety Disorders Association of Victoria Inc. (2014). Professional Development Workshop. Retrieved from https://www.adavic.org.au/product-view.aspx?Id=249

3. Beyond Blue (2016). Statistics and references. Retrieved from https://www.beyondblue.org.au/about-us/research-projects/statistics-and-references

4. Kearney, C & Albano, A. (2007). *When children refuse school: Assessment.* Oxford University Press.

Chapter 2

1. Field, E. M. (1999). B*ully busting: How to help children deal with teasing and bullying.* Sydney, Australia: Finch Publishing.

Chapter 6

1. Graham, L. (2013). *Bouncing back: Rewiring your brain for maximum resilience and well-being.* Novato, California: New World Library.

2. Samov, P.G. (2015). *Mindful Emotional Eating: Mindfulness Skills to Control Cravings, Eat in Moderation and Optimize Coping.* Pesi Publishing & Media.

Chapter 8

1. Woodcock, L., & Page, A. (2010). *Managing family meltdown: The low arousal approach and autism.* Dexter, MI: Jessica Kingsley Publishers.

CPSIA information can be obtained
at www.ICGtesting.com
Printed in the USA
BVHW061555160919
558546BV00025B/2337/P